Secrets of King's College Chapel

First published 2011
by Aeon Books
London NW3

www.aeonbooks.co.uk

British Library Cataloguing in Publication Data

A C.I.P. is available for this book from the British Library

ISBN-13: 978-190465-858-0

Secrets of King's College Chapel

Nigel Pennick

Aeon Books

Contents

St Gringoire says that he who sees and does not understand profits no more than he who hunts and catches nothing

– Jean Pucelle, *The Belleville Breviary* (c. 1319)

King's College Chapel, heraldic over the north door inside

Foreword

The Mysteries of King's College Chapel was my first published book, written in the years 1972 and 1973 and published in 1974. It was produced, published and printed by an independent local press that had emerged from a short-lived co-operative with which I was associated. This was the Cambridge Native Press, centred on the alternative newspaper, *Cambridge Voice.*

Founded by the doyen of the Cambridge alternative press scene, John Nicholson, The Land of Cokaygne, as it was called, was situated in a combined bookshop and printer's workshop at Jesus Terrace, on the edge of New Square, in the centre of the city. This bookshop was the first esoteric bookseller in Cambridge, covering the wide-ranging area that was then called 'Underground'. It recognized no distinction between radical politics ('town' rather than 'gown'), civil rights, ecology, art, 'alternative' culture, local folklore and history, and esoteric spirituality. It was John Nicholson who coined the rubric 'ancient skills and wisdom', which so aptly encapsulates the nature of the hidden heritage that underlies our culture. Among other 'firsts' to its name, Cokaygne was the first shop in Cambridge to stock Tarot cards, which, of course, can be bought widely to-day. A lot has changed since then.

Sadly, this press, bearing the name of the mythical English land of plenty, a visionary project for which its founder said 'I want to make a world which doesn't exist', was driven out of business by the political turmoil of 1974 and its accompanying three-day week. But before that disaster, Cokaygne achieved a flurry of creative publishing that included guides, local history studies (under the aegis of the Cambridge History Agency), the esoteric periodical *Arcana* and a number of 'underground' comics.

Cokaygne was seminal in bringing the concept of geomancy to the public's attention in Britain. In March 1973, the press published my influential booklet, *Geomancy*, and shortly afterwards it also published a centenary reprint of the Reverend E.J. Eitel's important 1873 work *Feng Shui, or The Rudiments of Natural Science in China*, with photographs by Ernst Borschmann and a foreword by John Michell. In the next year, *The Mysteries of King's College Chapel* saw the light of day, bringing the hidden esoteric roots of the chapel to public attention. It was reviewed in *The Times*, as well as the local press, and was well received.

The Mysteries of King's College Chapel appeared in 1974 and went out of print when The Land of Cokaygne was forced to close. Subsequently Thorsons of Wellingborough issued a new edition in 1978, and the Aquarian Press brought out a second impression of that edition in 1982. Although Cambridge booksellers stocked and sold it, the bookstall in King's College actually declined to sell it, apparently because it was deemed to be too critical of the changes wrought to the chapel by the college authorities in the 1960s. Since the late 1980s, it has been out of print, but much sought after.

In this new edition, *Secrets of King's College Chapel*, I have completely rewritten the original text, modifying it and adding certain material that, for economic reasons, I originally omitted from the previous editions, together with much new material that I have gained in the light of thirty years' further experience and research. Some of the original illustrations have been redrawn and there are photographs, including an archive one of 1867, which the original editions did not have.

Nigel Campbell Pennick
Cambridge, December 10, 2011

INTRODUCTION

The Chapel of King's College of Our Lady and St. Nicholas in Cambridge is as synonymous with Cambridge in the popular imagination as the Eiffel tower is with Paris, or the pyramids with Egypt. One view or another of King's College Chapel illustrates almost any publication dealing with Cambridge, from the telephone directory upwards. Even the City Council's logo is a drawing of the chapel. It is likely to be the one of the most photographed buildings in the city, and it has been recorded on film and video by thousands of the visitors who see it from the outside, and who daily stream through its portals.

In its commanding position, with its east end facing onto King's Parade and its west end visible from Queens' Road (The Backs), King's College Chapel can be seen from many parts of the town. Because, mercifully, tower blocks are banned in Cambridge, the chapel appears as part of the skyline when seen from vantage points outside the city. To the tourists who 'do' the chapel as a must-see attraction, it is frequently presented almost as an art gallery in which to admire *The Adoration of the Magi*, the renowned 1634 painting by Peter Paul Rubens. Naturally, as with all other churches on the tourist trail, it is a place in which to buy guidebooks, CDs of the much-admired choir and postcards, as well as less edifying souvenirs. At Christmas time, the traditional service of Nine Lessons and Carols is transmitted across the world from the chapel, and tickets to the event are much sought after.

In its long history, the chapel has been spared the iconoclastic blows of the Cromwellian puritan fanatic William Dowsing, lambasted in print by the Victorian architectural theorist John Ruskin, and, in the mid-20th century, drastically modified in order to highlight a valuable painting given to the college. But much earlier than that, the religious spirit of its founder was altered, first by King Henry VII's magnificent but temporal heraldic impress, and then by the Reformation and the stylistically different Renaissance art of the time of Henry VIII.

It seems to me, though, that in the many books that deal with so-called 'Gothic' architecture, King's College Chapel receives much less attention than it deserves, despite (or perhaps because of) its uniqueness. Apart from its remarkable constructional history, which gave it a notable unity of form, the chapel has the widest medieval fan-vaulting anywhere in existence, and the finest windows of Renaissance painted glass surviving in England.

King's College Chapel, from King's Bridge

CHAPTER 1

THE LOCATION, NATURE AND ACCESSIBILITY OF CAMBRIDGE

The City Name

Few cities are named after a bridge, so the very name of Cambridge attests to its importance as the crossing-point of the River Granta. The town was called Cambridge long before the river was known as the Cam, the name being a development (or corruption) of Grantebrycge and its variants – Granta bridge, from the original name of the river, Granta. From the tenth century until the time of Edward the Confessor, who died in 1065, coins were minted at Cambridge bearing the place-mark GRANT. The city's name is still Caergrawnt in modern Welsh.

Once the name Cambridge became established, people assumed that the bridge stood over a river called the Cam, and so it did. But the old name, Granta, never quite died. The bridge in question was once called The Great Bridge, but since the construction of several other bridges, it is now, usually, called Magdalene Bridge, after the nearby college.

Origins

In origin, Cambridge is a dual town. The original settlement appears to have been Roman, and to have borne the name of Durolipons. This was on the left bank, the north side of the river, and the street called Mount Pleasant follows the defensive ditch of part of the western and northern side. The north-south *cardo* of the Roman town is still in use, for it was the Roman road called the Via Devana, whose final objective was Chester. Until the nineteenth century, this part of the town was called The Borough. On the southern side of the river is the part of the town that was the main centre in medieval times, containing the market places and most of the historic churches and colleges. In early medieval times, the riverside on the right bank area, close to the Great Bridge known as the Holm (around the present St Clement's church), contained wharves of overseas traders, 'Irish Merchants' who may have been Danes from Dublin. In the year 878, Cambridge became part of the Danelaw. This Anglo-Danish town was burnt during the northern wars in the year 1010. The tower and some other parts of the oldest building in Cambridge, St Bene't's, dates from the reconstruction that followed.

Cambridge received a charter from King John in 1201, and the octocentenary was duly celebrated in 2001, ignoring the city's Romano-British, East Anglian, Mercian, Danish and Norman periods. Another foundation myth, relating to the Celtic period before the Romans, tells how Cambridge was an ancient British city called Caer Gwrgan, founded by a king of Britain called Gwrgan Varvtwch.

Until the nineteenth century, when legendary history was discounted as fanciful, or even fraudulent, certain antiquaries in the university attributed the town's foundation to the East Anglian King Sigebehrt in the year 643. But even though this

Magdalene Bridge – the original site of the Cam Bridge

has no documentary evidence, the town certainly existed long before the foundation of the university. This is conventionally dated to the founding of Peterhouse College in 1284, though scholars from Oxford were in the city from 1209.

St. Peter's Church, Cambridge

Sacred Locations in Cambridge

Little is known of religious places, save that local folklore asserts that the present church of St. Peter, off Castle Street, stands on the site of a temple of Diana. The fabric of the church, both Norman and later, contains Roman bricks. It appears that after the withdrawal of the Roman legions the city was abandoned. In Anglian times, a splendid marble sarcophagus, which was to hold the mortal remains of Aethelthryth (St. Etheldreda), foundress of the Abbey of Ely, was found by monastic agents at a ruined city called Grantacaestir. Round about the first millennium, Cambridge possessed a Minster, a monolithic cross that was found, in the nineteenth century, beneath the rampart of the castle bailey. As well as the undoubtedly Anglo-Saxon St. Benet's, built around the year 1025, there is evidence that the churches of St. Mary the Less, St. Botolph's, St. Edward's and St. Clement's, are also pre-conquest foundations.

Twenty-six years after the Norman Conquest, the first recorded monastic settlement in Cambridge took place. This was a house of Canons Regular, founded near to the Anglo-Saxon Minster which was in the vicinity of the castle. This house of Canons Regular became St. Giles' church when the monastery was moved to Barnwell in 1112, and there it remained, under Augustinian rule, until its dissolution in 1538. The present St. Giles' stands a little to the north of the Canons' church, which was demolished in the nineteenth century. Part of the churchyard was taken for road-widening in the early 1960s.

Other houses of religious orders in Cambridge were the Benedictine nunnery of St. Radegund, founded between 1133 and 1138 (dissolved on the petition of Bishop Alcock, Bishop of Ely, 1496), which is now Jesus College; the Gilbertine Priory of St. Edmund (destroyed); the Dominican Priory, for seventy friars, Cambridge being one of the four visitations into which the Dominican Province in England was divided (now Emmanuel College); the Franciscan Friary, founded around 1226 (now Sidney Sussex College); the Friars of the Penitence of the Lord Jesus Christ, commonly called the Friars of the Sack (taken over by Peterhouse College in 1307); the Carmelites; the Austin Friars; and the Pied Friars.

As well as these religious orders, Cambridge was connected with the *Fraternitas Sancti Sepulchri* (the Brotherhood of the Holy Sepulchre), who built the Holy Sepulchre, better known as the Round Church. It seems that, although the military order of the Knights Templar preferred the round form of church for their establishments, as in London, Temple Bruer and Northampton, the Cambridge round church was not one of theirs. It stood close to the Hospital of St. John the Evangelist, reflecting their namesakes' situation in Jerusalem. This area was, in fact, a ghetto known as the Jewry, for, before the deportation of the Jews on the order of the anti-Semitic

St. Bene't's Tower

King Edward I in 1290, Cambridge had one of the largest Jewish populations in England. There were two other hospital foundations in the environs of Cambridge, the hospital of St. Anthony and St. Eloy, and the leper hospital of St. Mary Magdalene at Barnwell (the still-extant Sturbridge Chapel).

The Port of Cambridge and Transport Links

From the above we can realise the continuing religious importance of Cambridge, which led the founders and foundresses of the various colleges to endow it with their establishments. Cambridge in the middle ages was one of the major inland ports of England, having a flourishing trade with mainland Europe and the Scandinavian ports of the North Sea. Sea-going vessels sailed up through the Fenlands, along the rivers to Cambridge, and unloaded their wares at numerous hithes, which at that time lined the easterly bank of the Cambridge river. The common known as Ships Green (now Sheep's Green) is a memory of the days when ship repairs were undertaken upon this piece of land. Sheep's Green is still a common, and is a continuation of the world-famous 'backs', the college gardens that at the time

Mill pool and boatyard

of the construction of King's College were part of the town commons, later appropriated by the colleges and university.

Despite its local importance, at the time of the foundation of King's College, the town of Cambridge was in the unique position of having no proper municipal rights. These had been taken away by royal decree in 1381, after an insurrection during which the townspeople had ransacked the university and burnt its charters and records. As a punishment to the townspeople, the university was accorded the powers and liberties normally granted to guilds and corporations, which the town did not regain until 1856. This lack of civic rights was an endemic cause of resentment against the university by the townspeople. This resulted in frequent disturbances and even riots, whenever the university exercised its power to the detriment of the town. Even after this nominal regaining of civic rights in 1856, eight unelected councillors nominated by the university sat in each town (later city) council until 1973, the town having finally received city status in 1951.

King's College Chapel from the former Milne Street

Before the founding of King's College, the area now occupied by the college buildings and King's Lawn was part of the dockland, a thriving trading area with houses, warehouses and inns, and its own church, St. John's Zachary (St. John the Baptist). At the east end of this church was what was then the main street of the town of Cambridge, called Milne Street. It ran roughly from south to north, parallel with High Street (now called King's Parade), from a point near the southern junction of the Anglo-Saxon King's Ditch with the river. At the point where Trinity College's Queen's Gate now stands, Milne Street turned east to join the High Street, the eastward extension of which was called St. Michael's Lane. From Milne Street lanes ran off to serve the riverside hithes, linking the focal point of town, the market, with the main transport facility. The market, serving both a port and the farming hinterland, had its own church, called St. Mary by the Market. Permanent stalls and lean-tos were built in the churchyard, which was really an extension of the market itself. This, too, was taken over by the university for its own use, and became Great St. Mary's, the 'University Church'. It was rebuilt at about the same time as King's College Chapel was constructed.

For the major part of its history, Cambridge's main communication with the outside world was by water. Until the construction of Denver Sluice in 1652 by the Dutch civil engineer Cornelius Vermuyden, the River Granta was tidal. An unimpeded passage for seagoing vessels was available from the open sea as far as the Mills (just upstream of the present Silver Street bridge). Because of the relative ease of transport so far inland, the town's environs became the venue for two of the most important fairs in Eastern England; the Midsummer Fair and the Sturbridge Fair, both chartered during the thirteenth century by King John. The Midsummer Fair is still the largest Cambridge fair, whilst Sturbridge petered out in 1933. Goods were brought in directly by water, and it was also by water that the stone and wood for the construction of the castle, town churches and university buildings arrived in Cambridge.

Before the construction of Denver Sluice, forty-ton barges could reach the town at high tide, but afterwards, to navigate the sluice, a new type of barge called the Fen Lighter was developed. It carried a mere fifteen tons. These carried sail, but near Cambridge, they were towed by horses or punted along with a pole. The pleasure punts of today are their descendents. Later, a causeway was built in the river where there were no longer riverside towpaths after the colleges had appropriated the riverbanks as their property. The horses pulling the barges then had to walk in the river.

During the nineteenth century, steam power was applied to river vessels, and this trade, carrying mainly timber and 'gas water' (waste from the gasworks to be recycled elsewhere for ammonia and coal tar) operated until about 1938. But by then, newer forms of transport had long since superseded water for the carriage of passengers, grain, coal, peat, bricks, stone and produce. In 1663, shortly after Vermuyden's canalization of the waterways as necessary for the drainage of the Fens, the first Act of Parliament for a new turnpike road to Cambridge was passed. Other roads quickly followed. Turnpikes meant stagecoaches, and in 1663 the first ran from the Devil's Tavern (on the site of the present Senate House) to London. After that, stagecoach transport expended rapidly and inns such as the Red Lion, Blue Boar, Eagle, Rose and Crown, Brazen George and Falcon were established.

But despite the success of stagecoaches, heavy haulage was still a problem between places that had no connection by river. By the late eighteenth century, canals were seen as the solution, and an act of Parliament was obtained for the construction of a canal to Cambridge from the existing Stort Navigation at Bishop's Stortford in Hertfordshire. Although the Act was given the Royal Assent, construction never commenced.

Later, the survey was put to another use, for in 1821, William James determined that the course assigned to the canal could equally be used for a railway. In April 1822 he sent a report of his findings to the Earl of Hardwicke. 'Having carefully surveyed the line selected for the proposed canal' he wrote, 'I can confidently state that the geological formation of the line of country is admirably adapted to the improved engine rail-road system by regular gradients, and that the powers given to the Company are ample for the construction ... and the work may immediately commence'.

The work did not immediately commence. Neither did a later 1825 proposal, by John and George Rennie, for a line up the Lee Valley to Cambridge. In the *London Gazette* of the 21st November 1834, another 'Railway or tram-road from the City of London to the Town of Cambridge' was proposed. Surveyed by Nicholas Wilcox Cundy, its route was via Bishop's Stortford. The station at Cambridge was to be located on the south side of the Huntingdon Road near to the present Storey's Way, the company being titled the Grand Northern and Eastern Railway. Again nothing happened. Successive transport proposals that result in much argument but no action is a theme still recognizable in twenty-first century Cambridge.

Between 1833 and 1844, various plans were prepared for rail lines. They were surveyed by, among others, Cundy, Joseph Gibbs, James Walker and John U. Rastrick. Finally, an extension of the Northern and Eastern Railway from Bishop's Stortford was proposed. In 1843 an act was passed for the line to be extended from Stortford to Newport. A further Act of 1844 authorized the building of the line 'From Newport by Cambridge to Ely and thence … to Brandon … and Peterborough'.

The Cambridge University authorities consistently impeded the construction of a railway station in an accessible part of the town. The station, as built, was located in the Middle Field of the Eastern Common Field that had been enclosed in 1807. It was, and is, a mile and a half from where most of the passengers wanted to go. Designed by Sancton Wood, Cambridge Station officially opened on the 29th of July 1845, and services began on the following day.

The Cambridge Railway Act included a clause that prohibited the taking up or setting down of rail passengers at the Cambridge Railway Station or at any place within three miles of it between ten in the morning and five in the afternoon on Sundays. This religiously-motivated by-law was copied from the Oxford Railway Act of 1843. In the Cambridge Act's provisions, infringement of this by-law was punishable by a fine not exceeding five pounds per passenger 'for the benefit of Addenbrooke's Hospital or other County charity to be decided by the University'. This was not the first, nor the last time that the university interfered with the town's commercial affairs. This regulation later prevented tramway operation in the streets of Cambridge on Sundays. In 1851, the issuing of cheap fares to Cambridge on Sundays for the seven o'clock morning train from Shoreditch terminal in east London caused the university vice-Chancellor to protest that these were 'as distasteful to the University Authorities as they must be offensive to Almighty God and to all right-minded Christians'. It is a notable Freudian slip that the vice-Chancellor considered the university's interests before those of the religion he was supposedly supporting.

All attempts at extending the railways further into Cambridge were resisted by the university, despite town approval. These included a line to Coe Fen (Cambridge and Lincoln Railway, 1844); near the Botanic Gardens (Cambridge and Oxford Railway, 1846; Royston and Hitchin Railway in 1847 and again in 1848; also the Cambridge and Shepreth Junction Railway in 1850); Queen's Road by the present Sidgwick Avenue

(Cambridge and Oxford Railway, 1846); the town gaol, which is now occupied by Queen Anne Terrace multi-storey car park (The Mayor's Committee, 1846); Silver Street (Royston and Hitchin Railway, 1851); Little St. Mary's Lane (Cambridge and Oxford Railway, 1846), and what would have been the most central of all, at Emmanuel Road, where Orchard Street joins it (Great Northern Railway, 1864). The final failure of the Great Northern Railway scheme of 1864 led the railway companies to give up the prospect of penetrating the town centre. Businessmen began to look for alternative methods of providing transport to the town centre from what was by then recognized as the only possible station. In 1880, horse trams were laid on, and after them, in 1914, motor buses provided public transport from the station to the town centre and the colleges. Even the trams and buses were subject to university interference, but that is another story.

During the twentieth century, especially after World War II (1939–45), a vast increase in motor traffic made a mockery of earlier university attempts to prevent mechanized transport from disrupting the contemplative academic calm of former times. If the shades of the long-dead dons who resisted the steam trains, Sunday travel, and later, the proposal to run electric trams along the Backs, could return by the power of some magus to twenty-first century Cambridge, they would be unable to comprehend the incessant stream of motor vehicles that now noisily throngs Queens' Road and the other streets each day of the week, including Sundays. They would have seen these machines as fouling the air, defiling nature, bringing noise and ugliness and desecrating the spiritual life. They would not have been wrong in viewing them in that way. But if the nineteenth century argument against trains had been conducted on grounds of ecology, humanity or spirituality, rather than the more easily dismissible university self-interest and sectarian religious dogma, would it have made any difference? Life has changed almost out of recognition from the way it was in pre-industrial times, and it is within the world-view of the pre-industrial that King's College Chapel originates.

Chapter 2

King Henry VI's Foundation

The Origin of King's College

On Passion Sunday, the 2nd of April 1441, the saintly King Henry VI founded King's College of St Nicholas of Bari, the patron saint of scholars, whose saint's day, 6th December, was also the King's birthday. King's College of St Nicholas originally had provision for a Rector and twelve scholars. The land for the college was conveyed to the king in January 1440/1, and the foundation stone was laid on Michaelmas Day (29th September 1441), by the Marquis of Suffolk on behalf of the king, who was only nineteen years of age at the time. The buildings were of three full storeys and work proceeded slowly, finally being finished in a makeshift manner (which lasted for three hundred and eighty years). The original college was expanded in 1443 into a society consisting of a Provost, seventy scholars, ten conduct priests (chaplains), six clerks, sixteen choristers and a master. Its name was the College Royal of Our Lady and Saint Nicholas of Cambridge.

The first chapel stood between the south side of the Old Court (the original foundation) and the north side of the present chapel, now a dark and secluded open space. It consisted of a chancel, nave and ante-chapel, a door at the west end, and east and west windows. These were presumably made of painted glass, since we know that in 1449 Henry VI brought John Utnyam from Flanders to make glass of all colours for Eton and the King's Colleges. The chapel was richly furnished. There are records of plate, hangings, relics, service books (illuminated manuscripts), vestments, choristers and both large and small organs. This original chapel was consecrated by the Bishops of Salisbury and Lincoln in 1443. The original overseer of the works, John Langton, was consecrated there as the Bishop of St. David's, on the 7th of May 1447.

By medieval standards of church construction, the original chapel was not very well built, for it fell down in 1537, having been in continuous use up to the eve of its collapse. It was clearly built in a hurry, after which it must have received little maintenance. A rise in the lawn on the north side of the present chapel marks the foundations of this original chapel. Services were transferred to the present chapel on the day the

King's College original entrance, now Old Schools

old one was wrecked. The necessary final work on the present chapel was carried out on the orders of King Henry VIII after the fall of the old chapel.

The new chapel (the present one) was begun after Henry VI's decision to enlarge the college. This resulted in the renaming of the college as King's College of Our Lady and St. Nicholas in Cambridge. The college was to admit no one but scholars from King Henry VI's other foundation, King's College of the Blessed Virgin Mary of Eton beside Windsor. Reflecting the custom of the age, they were exclusively male. Qualified scholars at Eton were first elected to scholarships, where they were taught logic and rhetoric. After three years of work they could proceed to a fellowship to study theology, though law, medicine and astronomy were also taught. King's College claimed independence from the university, and, in 1453, an order was issued, forbidding scholars to take their degrees until they had formally renounced university jurisdiction. Fellows and scholars had their hair cut, compulsorily, and, if they did not shave, their beards trimmed by the porter. Sporting in any form was forbidden, a notable contrast with the later strong emphasis on the value of sport in the public schools and universities.

King Henry had decided upon a chapel of cathedral dimensions (thirty-five feet longer than Oxford Cathedral) which naturally required an important location: one which the previous chapel had adjoined. There was a problem, because existing buildings occupied the proposed site, however by August 1443, the king had begun to acquire it. This new site was between High Street and the river, extending from Clare College southward to the house of the Carmelite Friars in the area west of Milne Street, and from the south boundary of Henry's original site about the same distance southwards in the area between Milne Street and High Street. This area incorporated a large part of Milne Street itself; Piron Lane, which connected Milne

Street to High Street, and two other lanes, Water Lane and Salthithe Lane, which led from Milne Street to the river.

Included in this area was the church of St. John's Zachary and its vicarage, on the axis of which was to be built the new chapel. St. John's Zachary was demolished in 1444 in anticipation of the commencement of construction. God's House, a collegiate institution for grammar teachers, which had been recently established at the corner of Piron Lane and Mime Street, was acquired along with two taverns and a number of houses. Kings had real power in the fifteenth century.

The important riverside salt hithe was acquired from the town, but a new way down to the river north of Trinity Hall was made by way of compensation. Then, in 1447, the King took from the town a large part of the commons on the other side of the river. These became the King's Backsides, now euphemistically shortened to 'the Backs'.

The Foundation and Royally-Stipulated Dimensions

The foundation stone was laid by His Majesty at the intended site of the high altar on St. James's Day, the 25th of July 1446. The laying of the foundation stone marked the extension of the axis of the dockland church of St. John's, eastward in an analogous manner to the chancel extensions at Canterbury

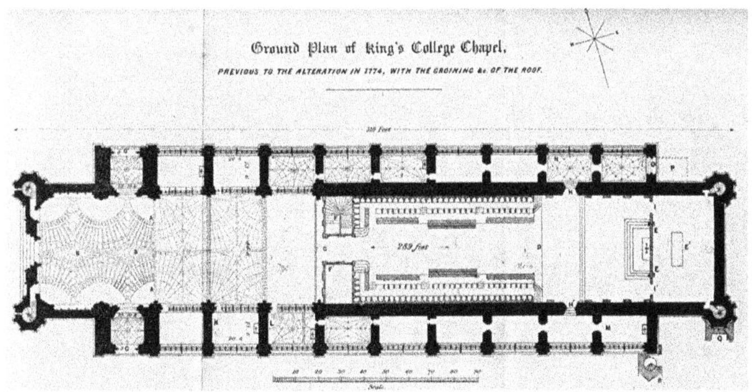

King's College Chapel plan, published 1867

Cathedral, Westminster Abbey and countless other churches. On the 2nd of November 1446 (All Souls' Day), the cemetery of the new college, which was, in reality, the old churchyard of St. John's Zachary, was consecrated by the Bishop of Norwich. An eastward extension is a common feature of most English cathedrals. In many cases this extra building is a chapel dedicated to Our Lady, the 'Lady Chapel'. King's College Chapel is itself equivalent to the eastward extension of the axis of St. John Zachary, and the chapel is dedicated to Our Lady.

Strangely, the foundation stone disappeared between the time of the foundation and the eighteenth century, when William Cole, the Cambridge antiquary, wrote: 'About 1770, when they dug the Foundations of the new Altar, they searched very minutely for this stone, according to this direction (ie. the founder's intent – N.P.); but to no purpose. I was there with Mr Essex the Architect more than once'.

The foundation stone was sited fourteen feet west of the middle of the future east wall in anticipation of the chapel's dimensions, as the part of land on which the extreme easterly end of the chapel was to stand was not purchased until 1451, three years after the king's will that set them forth. This will was not just a 'last will and testament' to be carried out on the death of the king, but a document for immediate action. The Will of Intent, written at Eton and dated 12th March 1447/8 gave detailed measurements for every part of the college:

> And as touching the dimensions of the church of my said college of Our Lady and Saint Nicholas of Cambridge, I have devised and appointed that the same church shall contain in length 288 feet of assize, without any aisles, and all of the wideness of 40 feet, and the length of the same church from the west end to the altar at the choir's door, shall contain 120 feet, and from the Provost's stall to the place called Gradus Chori [the choir step] 90 feet, for 36 stalls on either side of the same choir ….. and

from the said stalls to the east end of the said church 62 feet of assize. Also a reredos bearing the rood-loft ….. in length 40 feet and in breadth 14 feet; the walls of the same church to be in height of 90 feet, embattelled, vaulted, and charerofed [roofed with carpentry] sufficiently buttressed, and every buttress finished with finials: and in the east end of the said church shall be a window of 11 days (panels or 'lights'), and in the west end of the same church a window of 9 days, and betwixt every buttress a window of 5 days, and betwixt every of the same buttresses in the body of the church on both sides ….. a closet with an altar therein containing in length 20 feet and in breadth 10 feet vaulted and finished ….. and the pavement of the church to be enhanced (raised – N.P.) 4 feet above the ground outside and the height of the pavement of the choir 1 foot directly above the pavement of the church and the pavement at the high altar 3 feet above that. Item on the north side of the choir a vestry containing in length 50 feet, and in breadth 22 feet divided into two houses beneath and two houses above, which shall contain in height 22 feet in all, with a vaulted entry from the choir. Item at the west end of the church a cloister square the east pane (wing) containing in length 175 feet, and the west pane as much: and the north pane 200 feet, and the south pane as much: of the which the ambulatory 14 feet wide, and in height 20 feet to the corbel table, with clerestories and buttressed with vaulted and embattled finials and the ground (level) thereof 4 feet lower than the church ground; and in the middle of the west pane of the cloister a strong square tower, containing 24 feet within the walls, and in height 120 feet to the corbel table, and 4 small turrets over that finished with pinnacles, and a door into the said cloister ward, and outward none.

The dimensional part of the king's will was finished by the following exhortation/curse:

> And that this my said will in every point before rehearsed may the more effectually be executed I not only pray and desire but also exhort in Christ, require and charge all and every of my said feoffees, my executors and surveyor or surveyors in the virtue of the aspersion of Christ's blessed blood and of His painful passion that they having God and my intent only before their eyes, not letting for fear or favour of any person living of whatever estate, degree or condition, that he may truly faithfully and diligently execute my same will, and every part thereof, as they will answer before the blessed and dreadful visage of our Lord Jesus in his most fearful and last doom when every man shall be examined most narrowly and deemed after his demerits (receive just reward for his failings). **(Bracketed explanatory notes are by Nigel Pennick; the English and numerals are modernized).**

Thomas John Proctor Carter comments on this last section in his *King's College Chapel: Notes on its History and Present Condition* (1867): 'A sad and almost prophetic foreboding of future troubles must have prompted these awfully solemn words, the very stringency of which only serves to remind us how powerless such appeals are wont to be'. Henry was born at Windsor in the year 1421. A story about his birth tells that when his father, Henry V, was informed that Catherine had borne him an heir he asked: 'where was the boy born?' 'At Windsor' was the reply. Turning to his Chamberlain, he made the following prophetic statement: 'I Henry born at Monmouth, shall small time reign, and much get; but Henry of Windsor shall long reign and lose all. But as God will, so be it.' If this story is not just apocryphal, the fatalism of Henry VI may originate with his father's prophecy.

The royally-defined measurements of the chapel are thus: length two hundred and eighty-eight feet; width forty feet; height of the walls ninety feet; ceiling eighty feet; pavement four feet above ground level; choir pavement five feet above ground level; high altar pavement eight feet above ground level. Subsequent to his untimely death, the detailed plans given by the king were followed almost to the letter by architects, leading to the chapel's completion substantially as designed. Clearly, the plans drawn up by the original draughtsmen were preserved by the college during the long breaks in construction. The only significant departures from the royal plans for the chapel were the omission of the vestry and the construction of the east window with nine instead of eleven panels (which Carter (1867) surmises may have been XI as a mistake for the Roman IX anyway). The cloister and tower were never begun.

Chapter 3

Building the Chapel

> To the honour of Almighty God, in whose hand are the hearts of Kings; of the most blessed and immaculate Virgin Mary, mother of Christ; and also of the glorious Confessor and Bishop Nicholas, Patron of my intended College, on whose festival we first saw the light.
>
> **Dedication by King Henry VI**

Design and Craftsmanship

When the question of who actually designed the chapel is addressed, the initial concept, that is the ground-plan and dimensional lay-out, definitely stems from King Henry VI, himself following Roman Catholic tradition. As Geoffrey de Vinsauf observed in his Poetria Nova, written around the year 1210: 'If a man has to lay the foundations of a house, he does not set his hands to work in a hurry. It is the inner line of the heart that measures out the work in advance. The inner man works out a definite scheme of action. The hand of the imagination designs everything before the body performs the act. The pattern is first the idea, then the physical reality'

Sacred measure is a constant theme both in ancient Jewish tradition and in the temples of the gods of Greece and Rome. Medieval Christian architecture has elements that are derived from both of these traditions, as well as from the carpentry of ancient northern Europe. The Tabernacle of the Israelites, designed by Bezazel and Aholiab, was a complex ritual structure of timber, precious metal and textiles, constructed according to a system of proportion in which the ratio 26:15 appears. The proportions recorded in scriptural accounts, as well as numerical and geometrical traditions received through the works of Pythagoras, Euclid and Vitruvius, were influential in the symbolic designs of Christian sacred places. The dimensions given by King Henry VI for his chapel are concerned largely with internal measures, for it is these that define the sacred space within. Thus, the building is treated as an interior space, literally, a sacred vessel. Sacred dimensions of buildings given in Biblical texts define the inner spaces: Solomon's 'House of the Lord', the House of the Forest of Lebanon and the 'Holy of Holies' of Ezekiel's vision. External dimensions are given for smaller liturgical paraphernalia; the Ark of the Covenant, the Altar of Full Offering and the acacia wood table. The measurements of Noah's Ark have usually been seen as referring to the internal dimensions of the symbolic vessel.

Of the actual implementation of the chapel concept, Reginald Ely 'Master Mason of Our College Royal', appointed by a Patent of Henry VI 'to press masons, carpenters and other workers' was the equivalent of to-day's architect who brings the patron's requirements into physical reality. When the chapel was built, all work was done by hand by skilled craftsmen who had been through traditional training. In medieval Europe, organized craft practice had three stages: apprentice, journeyman and master. These correspond to the three stages

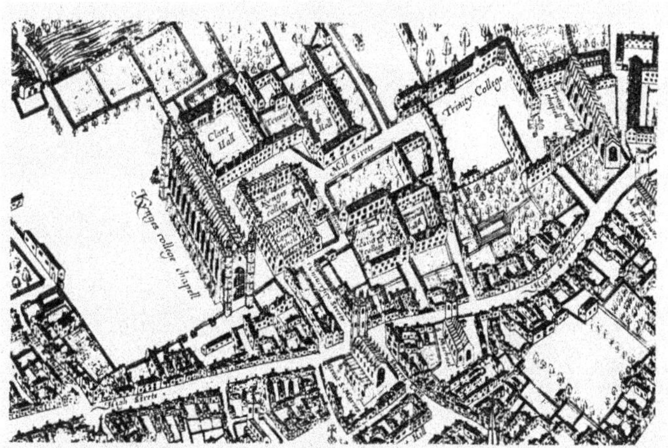

King's College Chapel Cambridge, 17th century

of learning. First, the novice has spontaneity without control. In the next stage, the craftsman has learnt control, but with the loss of spontaneity. The third stage, masterhood, consists of having control with spontaneity. Once the journeyman has reached this stage, he can produce his 'masterpiece' for judgement by a panel of masters, and then, if it is up to standard, he too becomes a master craftsman. Until the nineteenth century in Great Britain, all masters, journeymen and apprentices were governed by the guild of their trade. The guilds set the standards of work, awarded masterships, governed fair prices and set the going rates of pay for journeymen.

Craftsmanship in northern Europe goes back to the most ancient times, long before the medieval period, and before the Roman occupation. The development of particular currents of craftsmanship may well come from the practices of particular families or castes in prehistoric times. Among the earliest recorded ancient craftsmen are the smiths. From linguistic studies, it appears that in early times, the word smith was used not only for the forgers of metal, but for craftsmen working with all kinds of materials. The Old Norse word *smithr* meant not only a handworker, but also master builder. Smith is still one of the more common names in Great Britain, and equivalents in other European languages show the same frequency. In medieval Scotland and the north of England, all men who worked with the hammer were deemed to be 'hammermen', and members of the Hammermen's Guild. For example, in 1694 the hammermen of Selkirk in Scotland included blacksmiths, coopers, a coppersmith, stonemasons and wrights. Thus the traditional crafts have always been interlinked, though in practice, the various craft skills were strictly demarcated from one another by the guilds.

The Articles and Points of Masonry, preserved in an English manuscript from around 1430, sets out the duties and rights of the mason. It is divided into two lists of nine precepts, the first of which is concerned with the conduct of the master, and the second with the mason serving under him. They emphasise honesty, morality, diligence, supportiveness and solidarity. These second nine are as follows:

> It behoves him first to acknowledge God and the Holy Church and all the Saints, and his master and his fellows as his own brethren. The second point, he must fulfill his day's work truly for which he takes his pay. The third, that he heed the council of his fellows in the lodge, and in the chamber, and in every place where they are as masons. The fourth point, that he do no disservice to the aforesaid art, neither prejudice nor give support to any articles against the skill nor against any of the art, but he shall support it with all honour as much as he can. The fifth point, when he shall take his pay, he shall take it meekly at the time ordered by the master for it and that he fulfill the stipulations of work and of his rest as ordered and fixed by the master. The sixth point, if any discord shall arise between him and his fellows, he shall obey his master meekly and be still at the bidding of him or of the warden of his master, in his master's absence, until the following holy day and that he agree then to the disposition of his fellows and not upon the work days hindering their work and the profit of his lord. The seventh point, that he covet not the wife or the daughter of his master, or of another of his fellows unless it be for the marriage, nor keep concubines because of the discord that might befall among the fellows. The eighth point, if it befall him to be warden under his master that he be true between his master and his fellows and that he be busy in the absence of his master to the honour of his master and to the profit of the lord he serves. The ninth point, if he be wiser and more subtle than his fellows

> working with him in his lodge or in any other place and he perceives that this fellow should leave the stone that he is working on for want of cunning, and if he can teach him and improve the stone, he shall tell him and help him that more love may increase among them and that the work of the lord be not lost. **(English modernized by Nigel Pennick).**

It was by men following these precepts that King's College Chapel was built.

Construction of the Chapel

King Henry VI stipulated that the whole work of construction was to be committed to the supervision of William Wayneflete, Bishop of Winchester. The king also stipulated that the wages of the workmen should be as follows: £50 per annum (at that time a top person's salary) for the master of works; £13 6s 8d for the clerk of works; £16 3s 4d for the chief mason; £12 8s for the chief carpenter, and £6 3s 4d for the chief smith.

The chapel was built in three distinct and separate phases, reflecting the uncertain and turbulent times. Most of the original money used by King Henry VI to pay for the first phase was obtained by the seizure of cells of foreign abbeys authorized by a Papal Bull of 31st January 1448/9. The initial period of construction took place from the foundation, in 1446, until 1461. This was under the direction of the Master Mason Reginald Ely, during which time part of the eastern end was completed. During this first period of construction, the first general supervisor was John Langton, Chancellor of Cambridge university (although King's claimed independence from that body, Langton was one of the original six members of King's and subsequently became Bishop of St. David's, being consecrated in the old chapel). For a short period in 1447, he was followed by William Millington. Next was the Flemish cleric Nicholas Cloos, another of the original six, sometime curate of St. John's Zachary. He retained the post of supervisor after his consecration as Bishop of Carlisle on March 14th 1449/50. Subsequently, Cloos was made Bishop of Lichfield (August 31st 1452). After Cloos' death in the same year, Robert Woodlarke, the Provost of King's, was appointed in December 1452.

During this first period, up until 1461, when work ceased on the overthrow of King Henry, Reginald Ely was master mason. In the next ten years, until his own death in 1471, Ely was no longer connected with the construction of the chapel. In this pre-1461 period, the warden of the masons was John Brown. Thomas Sturgeon was master-carpenter, being named in impressment commissions both in 1443 and 1449. The name Sturgeon has a later connection with the construction of the chapel, when, in 1480, John Sturgeon, possibly Thomas's son, and Martin Prentice received letters patent for the transport by water of timber for the chapel roof. In 1449, Henry VI brought a Flemish glass master, John Utnyam, from the Low Countries to make glass for King's College, but, so far as is known, none ever reached the present chapel.

King's College Chapel, west end detail

Constructionally, the chapel itself has walls of brick faced with ashlar, and incorporating a 'damp-course' of oyster shells. Before 1461, construction utilized stone from Thefdale (Jackdaw Crag or Petres Post) Quarry, one and a half miles south of Tadcaster in Yorkshire. Possession of this quarry was granted to the college in 1447. Stone was available from the Huddleston Quarry by 1446, and from King's Cliffe Quarry in Northamptonshire by June 1460. King's Cliffe was also the quarry from which the stone for Trinity College Great Gate and fountain was obtained. Before 1452, King's College had also acquired a clunch (chalk) quarry at Hinton (now Cherry Hinton, a suburb of Cambridge). Excepting that from Hinton, which was carted, all stone was carried by water to Cambridge.

The period during which Henry was building the chapel was a time of trouble; the civil war known now as The Wars of the Roses. The king himself, being a devout Christian, was a pacifist, and would not fight, although he appeared in person on the battlefield. After he was taken prisoner at the battle of St. Albans (23rd of May 1455), having been wounded in the

King's College Chapel, side chapel vault

neck with an arrow, the work slowed down, although Robert Woodlarke, Cloos' successor, writes: 'When Henry VI was taken prisoner by the Earls of Salisbury and Warwick they pledged their word to him, in order to gain his good will, that they would hasten the completion of his church and all other building operations in Cambridge'.

During the lengthy construction, even after the death of Henry VI, the original plans were rigidly adhered to, following the Ninth Article from the first nine precepts (the masters' duties) of *The Articles and Points of Masonry*: 'The ninth article is this, that no master shall supplant another, for it is said that in the art of masonry that no man can bring to an end so well the work begun by another to the profit of his lord as he that began it, unless it be by his designs or by him to whom he shows his designs.'

Work, in fact, continued, and the two north-easterly side chapels were completed at the time of the overthrow of the king, who had by then retreated to the north of England. He was defeated at the battle of Towton Moor on the 29th of March 1461, one of the bloodiest battles ever fought on English soil, in which 36,000 were killed. Then Edward IV reigned in his stead. In 1465, Henry was captured again and imprisoned in the Tower of London. He was released and restored to the throne briefly in September 1470 when Edward fled to Flanders. Edward returned a few months later with a task force of Burgundian soldiers, defeated Henry at Tewkesbury, and killed his son. Henry was once again imprisoned. On the 21st of May 1471, at the age of forty-nine, the ex-king was murdered in the Tower, his body being taken rapidly from London and buried hastily at Chertsey Abbey.

The two side-chapels completed under the supervision of Reginald Ely are vaulted with lierne vaulting, so called because the ribs of the vault fancifully resemble 'lierne' (ivy). This lierne vaulting bears numerous claves (roof bosses) with figurative carvings. They include Christ enthroned in majesty, flanked by two angels; an eagle killing another bird; bearded human faces; a head surrounded by a two-banded twist pattern, perhaps representing a rope (Judas Iscariot or a Masonic intitiation?), and a face with leafy branches of oak emanating from the mouth.

Work effectively came to a halt in 1471 when Henry was murdered by his oath-breaking captors. But some workmen

King's College Chapel, side chapel vault

were still employed in maintaining the unfinished structure. On the 23rd of October 1467 the 'towers of the new church' were covered in to protect the stonework from the ravages of frost. In 1472, the masons' lodge, first mentioned in a document of 1467, was rebuilt. The site of this is unknown. In 1476, a receipt of donations *pro fabrica nove ecclesia* (on behalf of the fabric of the new church) marked the recommencement of work on a serious scale. In 1477, £10 19s 4d was collected from the fellows of the college to continue the work. In that year, John Bell, Warden of the Masons, was sent to Huntingdon to buy stone. Other consignments of building stone were purchased from Peterborough and Clipsham (Rutlandshire). In 1479, Walter Field succeeded Woodlarke. During Field's Provostship, between January the 10th 1480/1, and June the 14th 1483, receipts from the construction were £1,240, and a further consignment of stone was purchased, this time from Weldon, Hesilborough.

During this second major phase of construction, in 1476, John Wolrych, who had been an ordinary free mason on Old Court in 1443, became Master Mason. Simon Clerk of St. Edmundsbury succeeded him in 1477. He was also engaged on

King's College Chapel, south side

the construction of Saffron Walden church, in Essex. Martin Prentice, first known to be connected with the chapel in 1459, became master carpenter in 1480, and ceased to work on the project before 1486. In 1480, the smiths working on the iron-work for the second window on the south side were Smith Kendal and Andrew Hacon.

Funding for the chapel during the second period was as follows: King Edward IV contributed £1,113 6s 8d; Thomas Rotherham, Bishop of Lincoln, Chancellor of England and another of the six original members of King's College, £100; King Richard III £750. In August 1484, King Richard III ordered the removal of the body of King Henry VI from Chertsey, where it had been ignominiously interred, to a new tomb to the south of the High Altar in St. George's Chapel, Windsor. Many miracles were reported taking place at the tomb of the King, but despite it becoming an object of pilgrimage and veneration, two attempts to make Henry VI into a saint failed. The coffin of the King was opened, in the presence of members of King's College, in 1910, and a piece of silk was taken from the cloth in which the King's bones were wrapped, a relic preserved to this day at the college.

Richard III, in reverence to the late King Henry, accelerated the building works, but his death at the battle of Bosworth in 1485 brought it all to a halt. Under Richard III, glass was bought for the east window, the north-east and the south-east side windows. The south-east window was only half a window, the lower half having a planned building abutting onto it. William Neve, the King's Glazier, and John Byrchold, the King's Sergeant Plumber, visited the chapel at the end of 1484 to supervise the glazing of these windows.

Roof Construction

Oaks for roofing the completed portion were brought from far afield. It was transported to Cambridge from Canfield Park, Bardfield, Sapley, Stansted Park, Thaxted, Walden and

Weybridge. With this timber, the carpenters erected a roof over the first five bays of the chapel, which by then had been completed. Compass-drawn early-style Arabic numerals can still be seen on the roof trusses, numbered one to six (1480s) and one to eight (later), these being among the earliest use of them in English building construction. Until the eighteenth century moss was to be seen on the weathered western sides of the fifteenth pair of principals from the west end, which was left open to the riverside weather for twenty years at this period.

The roof is made up of 24 bays demarked by pairs of principals with wall-posts, cambered collar-beams and curved braces running from wall-posts to collars to form four-centred arches. The posts and braces continue against the piers as far down as the vaulting, but in the intermediate trusses, which are four feet wider, they are not so long, ending approximately two feet below the wall-plate. The rafters are laid flat. They are supported by two purlins on each side, each reinforced by wind-braces.

The carpentry work is very fine. All secondary timbers are chamfered (the work of Martin Prentice is distinguishable from the later carpentry by double chamfering). When the roof was leaded, firewood from the market was found to

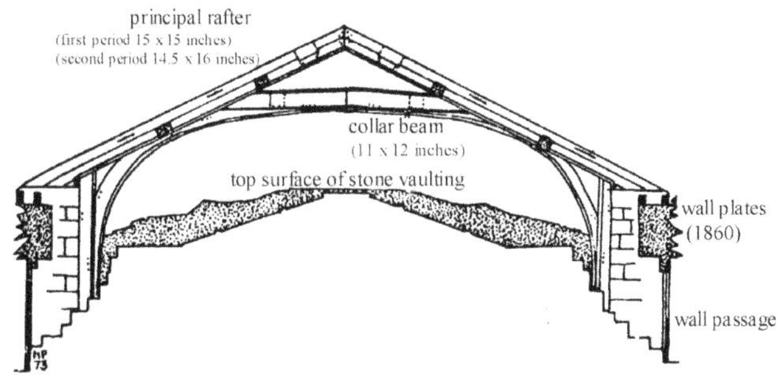

King's College Chapel, roof-truss section

King's College Chapel roof

be too expensive, and wood was brought from Walden Park along with the roof-beams. According to H. Malden (1769), no spiders have ever appeared, nor has any cobweb ever been seen on any of the roof beams. Between 1861 and 1863, Giles Gilbert Scott oversaw remedial work in the roof that included the insertion of wrought iron tie-rods and re-leading.

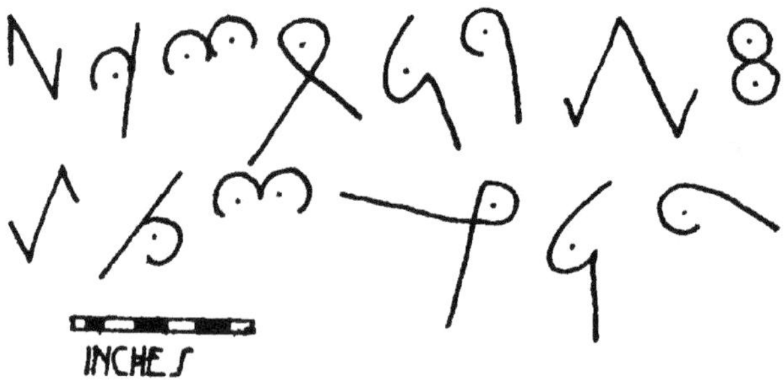

King's College Chapel, Arabic numerals in roof

Completion of the Stonework

At the defeat and death of Richard III in 1485, the chapel was complete as far as the fifth bay westward. This part of the chapel was roofed, but unvaulted. The brick walls, which were eventually intended to be covered up when the vaulting was erected, rose higher than the ashlar facing inside, so they were painted white to reduce their conspicuousness. Without end towers, pinnacles or crenellations, the entrance to the chapel was by a door on the south side, in the fifth side-chapel westward, which was completed in June 1480.

Work ceased in 1485, and Clerk died four years later. Work on the chapel did not resume in earnest until 1508, when King Henry VII granted £1,500 towards its completion. Work resumed in full swing in March 1508/9, when master mason

King's College Chapel, angel musicians, south side

John Wastell was appointed at a salary of £13 6s 8d per annum. The 'comptroller' at this time was William Swayne, succeeded in 1509 by John Lee. Harry Semerk was warden of the masons.

John Wastell was one of the leading architects of his day. Between 1493 and 1505, he designed and oversaw the construction of the 'Bell Harry' or 'Angel' tower at Canterbury Cathedral, the mother church of England, on the orders of Prior Goldstone. Wastell also designed the eastern chapels at Peterborough Cathedral, and the porch and pinnacles of Saffron Walden church (after 1485). The Saffron Walden pinnacles are virtually identical with those on King's College Chapel. Wastell also constructed the Great Gate of Trinity College

King's College Chapel, side chapel head boss

King's College Chapel, east end

(1491-92, 1496-97), whose wall-panelling over the small arch is identical with that on the Canterbury tower. Wastell is likely to have designed the Great Gate of St. John's College (1511-16), where typically Wastellian fan vaulting was used.

In his fifty-second year, when he discovered that he was suffering from consumption (tuberculosis, then a terminal illness), the hitherto miserly Henry VII decided to spend his money on charitable works. On the 24th of March 1508/9, among other benefactions, he gave the college £5,000. The deed of conveyance stipulated that it was to be used entirely for building and finishing the chapel 'after like for, and intent as it was ordered and devised by our uncle' (Henry VI), without discontinuing or ceasing the work so far as the money would allow, and, if not completed during his lifetime, additional funds would be provided from his estate by his executors.

From 1509 to 1515, Richard Russell was master-carpenter. He constructed the last seven bays of the timber roof exactly to the pattern set by Prentice, with the exception of the double chamfering. Russell's principals have a single stop-chamfer. Plumbers completed the roof-leading between April and December 1512.

Between October 1512 and August 1513, stone carvers were employed in the chapel. Thomas Stockton, the king's joiner, was master carver from 1509 to 1515, and received an annual salary of £18 5s 0d. Putting a joiner in charge of the stone carving explains how woodcarving techniques were used to create the stone heraldic symbols in the ante-chapel. It is an example of the overlap in trades that occasionally occurred in prestigious projects (another being the making of the dragon weathervane on St Mary le Bow church in London in 1679).

These heraldic devices were the first deviation away from the hitherto purely sacred character of the chapel, as intended by the founder, and towards the secular pomp beloved of the Tudors. In the first two periods, the carving in the chapel had no secular content except a single instance of the Royal Arms of England. In the later period, heraldry ran rife, on both the interior and exterior walls. However one of the Tudor Roses, on the west end towards the south, has a small female figure

King's College Chapel, side chapel vault

in the middle of it. Henry Malden wrote of it in 1759 as 'a small figure of the Virgin Mary: after which foreigners make frequent enquiries, and never fail to pay it a religious reverence; crossing their breasts at the sight, and addressing it with a small prayer'. The heraldic beasts on the westerly buttresses originally had iron brackets on which to hang banners, which were flown from them on state occasions, as King's was, after all, a royal foundation.

Chapter 4

Finishing the Chapel

The Fan Vaulting

One of the most magnificent features of the chapel is the lace-like stone fan vaulting, which never ceases to impress first-time visitors. On the 8th of February 1511/12, £5,000 was granted to the college by the executors of the king's will, on condition that it was to be vaulted according to 'the form of a plat'. In 1512, John Wastell commenced the vaulting, in Weldon Stone, costing £100 per severy (bay), the time stipulated being three years for completion of the twelve. Geometrically, the masterly fan vaults are in the form of rectangular portions of the four quadrants of an inverted concave conoid, mitred into one another at their junctions.

Fan vaults appear to have been developed as skeuomorphic replicas of textile hangings suspended as a tabernacle over coffins during lyings-in-state and funerals. Hung from posts erected at the four corners of the catafalque, a wish to make them more permanent seems to have led to these pall-cloths being reproduced in other, more durable, materials. Where the custom originated is not known, but it seems to have been some time in the thirteenth century. A notable stone tabernacle of this kind was made at Tewkesbury for Sir Hugh Despenser, who died in 1349. Wooden ones were also made. One was installed over the tomb of Edward, the Black Prince, in Canterbury Cathedral (1376).

Fan vaults were not new when Wastell decided to use them, having been around in some form or other for two centuries. The technique was developed by the royal masons and first used in 1292 at St Stephen's Chapel, Westminster (destroyed in 1834). Later, it appeared in the Chapter House of Old St Paul's Cathedral (1332, destroyed 1666). The oldest surviving example of English fan vaulting is in the cloisters of Gloucester Cathedral, dated between 1370 and 1412.

By the end of the fifteenth century, however, masons had developed and refined fan vaulting far beyond the early versions, making it the state-of-the-art in masonry. The first

King's College Chapel, vaulting 3

large fan vaults were built in the 1440s in the presbytery of Sherborne Abbey in Dorset. The fan vaults of the choir and transepts of Bath Abbey (1499), designed by William Vertue, are almost identical with Wastell's in King's College Chapel. The retro-choir at Peterborough Cathedral was built with fan vaults by Wastell before he finished King's College Chapel.

Fan vaulting, taken from the nearby Augustinian abbey and dated 1508, exists in Circencester, in the chapel of St Katherine, and Abbot Lichfield's chantries in the churches of All Saints' and St Lawrence in Lichfield are dated 1514 and 1539. Also subsequent to King's College Chapel, very similar fan vaulting was erected over the south aisle in the parish church of Cullompton, Devon in 1529. Some of these vaults were erected over tombs, or, during their development, chantry chapels. Others were not funereal in meaning, and perhaps these were viewed as reproducing the tabernacle of the Israelites in the wilderness.

According to Malden, the chapel clerk, writing in 1759: '... this roof is so geometrically contrived, that it would stand firm without either the walls or the key stone' (i.e. supported only by the buttresses and end towers – N.P.) 'The mystery of constructing vaults of this kind was the original secret of the Free-Masons: of whom John Wastell, the Master-Mason, contracted to employ not less than sixty, for carrying on the works of this chapel.'

In fact, fan vaulting was built with no central keystone at all in the tower at Fotheringhay church in Northamptonshire, where a circular aperture boarded with wooden planks is at its centre. The fan vaulted interior of the Bell Harry Tower at Canterbury, designed by Wastell, is similar, having a stone roundel like a blind rose window at its centre (circa 1504). Sir Christopher Wren draws on this Bell Harry Tower vault at St Mary Aldermary in London (1682), which has flattened 'saucer domes' between fan vaulting.

King's College Chapel, main vault

Because Reginald Ely designed the internal structure of the chapel to have a more pointed form of vaulting, with the ribs arising at a lower point that the flatter fan vaulting, Wastell had to construct panelling above the windows in order to preserve the internal dimensions stipulated by the founder, keeping the ceiling height at the crown at eighty feet. The centres of the fan vaulting are composed of twelve large claves ('central keys' or 'keystones'). They are carved alternately with Tudor Roses and Portcullises sculpted by Thomas Stockton. They hang two feet six inches below the apex of the vault, and are three feet five inches in diameter. On the top there is a 'square piece in the centre, where the lewis, or whatever other machine was used for the purpose of lowering the key into its place, is supposed to have been inserted' (F. Mackenzie, *Observations on the Construction of the Roof of King's College Chapel*, 1841).

Having taken the completion of the vaulting in hand, Wastell was contracted in January 1512/13 to make twenty-one buttress finials 'accordyng to the fynyall of oon buttrasse which is wrought and sett up; except that all thies new fynyalles shal be made sumwhat larger in certain places acordyng to the mooldes for the same conceyvid and made'. This contract infers a kind of optical device, akin to that of the ancient Greek *entasis*, which makes part of a building, or a whole building appear 'square' in perspective, as in the best Classical buildings. *Entasis* can be seen well in the pillars of the neoclassical buildings of Downing College, including those designed by Quinlan Terry in the 1980s and 90s. The northwest turret was completed at the same time as the finials. This medieval optical device can no longer be checked, as the pinnacles were totally reconstructed in 1754, and further repaired in 1811 and 1875. They were patched up early in the twentieth century, and replaced by new work in the 1970s. The end parapets were originally of a slightly different form, if the watercolour by J.M.W. Turner and the engraving by Harraden are accurate records of the chapel's west end at their time.

In March 1512/13, a third contract was made between the college and John Wastell for three more towers to be made

King's College Chapel interior, 1867

to match the first. Of the easternmost, this meant only the turret; for the westward, it meant parts of the towers and the turrets. These octagonal turrets are in six stages, with pilaster-like projections at the free corners, rising from pedestal bases superimposed on the main plinth, giving the effect of interpenetration of the plinth-mouldings through the pedestal. The top of each turret, which is divided into two stages, rises free above the main parapet, the corner projections continuing through it as pinnacled standards. The faces of the octagon between the standards are filled with a latticework of pierced stone in the form of open quatrefoils in diagonal squares. These were described in Wastell's contract as 'cross-quarters'. The pinnacles of the standards and the crenellated parapets that link them form a corona round a crowning octagonal turret. This turret has a domical ogee crocketed cap of ashlar raised on a high drum pierced with quatrefoiled circles. Carved in high relief on the eight faces of the cap are alternate crowned portcullises and Tudor roses.

The turrets of King's College Chapel are the focus of an interesting historical controversy. Loggan's print of 1688 clearly shows a lightning conductor on the finial of each of the four ogee crocketed caps. When they were installed is not recorded. But the invention of lightning conductors is frequently ascribed (always by American historians) to Benjamin Franklin, who lived a century later. Clearly, either he copied already existing examples, or, in ignorance, reinvented the lightning conductor.

A fourth contract stipulated, in August 1513, the vaulting of two porches, seven side-chapels, another nine side-chapels 'behind the quire', and all the crenellations of the porches and chapels. The vaults were to be finished by midsummer 1514 at a cost of twenty-five pounds for the porches, and twenty pounds and twelve pounds each respectively for the elaborate and plainer vaults. In 1515, the year Wastell seems to have died, the chapel's stonework got as far as it ever would. Completion of the stonework had taken sixty-nine years in all. All that was left for the masons to complete was the screen. They made abutments for it, but no more was done. Later, when King Henry VIII was finally convinced that he should allocate some money towards the chapel, a carved wooden screen, in Renaissance style, was installed.

King's College Chapel, interior

The Renaissance choir-stalls and wooden screen in King's College Chapel attest to the total alteration in outlook during King Henry VIII's regime, when the Protestant Reformation culminated in the closure of six hundred and forty-five monasteries, the suppression of two thousand three hundred and seventy-four chantries and free chapels, one hundred and ten hospitals and ninety colleges, and the commencement of the seizure of the common lands from the yeomen of England. The preaching of the Word in plain buildings was substituted for gorgeous religious images, stunning colour and the sumptuous rites and ceremonies of Catholicism. So King's College Chapel was never finished as the founder and architects planned.

Spiritual and Symbolic Colour

The original intention of the designers was to paint the interior, the normal practice at the time, blending the numerology, heraldic and symbolic colour, dimensions, incenses, music, rites and ceremonies in an earthly expression of the unimaginable splendour of God. This medieval Christian total work of art

King's College Chapel, pinnacle

was a spiritual device that created a true cosmic consciousness in those who participated. The present puritanical interior is but a pale shadow of the masterful artistry that was envisaged by its architects. Each rib of the vault was to be coloured Gules (scarlet), and the fan-background Azure (blue). Gilded stars were to grace this heavenly blueness, and the vaulting ribs between were to be outlined with gold. The whole scheme paraphrases Nature, seeing the chapel's pillars as trees, and the tracery-bars as branches with stars visible between them.

An idea of the planned splendour of the painted interior can be had by visiting those remaining medieval churches whose

King's College Chapel, corner tower pinnacle from roof

painted interiors have survived, or been faithfully restored. The total scheme is visible today, in miniature, in the Chantry of Bishop Goldwell (d. 1499) at Norwich Cathedral.

Proper heraldic colours were to have graced the royal coats of arms of the chapel, and polychrome figures of saints were to have been erected in the tabernacles. The painting and embellishing was never implemented, owing first to lack of funds and then to the end of Catholic worship in England. The painters only got to work on one small chapel on the south side, where traces of paint can still be seen.

The spiritual and symbolic meaning of colour in medieval England is recorded in several documents dealing with Anglo-Norman heraldry. Notably, these are Anselm's *Palais de'Honneur*; a manuscript of the time of King Edward III, *Enseignement Notables aux poursuivants*; and the fifteenth century *Boke of St Albans* by Dame Juliana Berners. Berners describes the divine origin of this system. 'The lawe of arms the which was effigured and begun before any lawe in the worlde, both the lawe of nature and before the commandments of God. And this lawe of arms was grounded upon the nine diverse orders of angels in heaven encrowned with nine diverse precious stones of colours and of virtues diverse also of them are figured the nine colours in arms' (partly modernized English spelling – N.P.)

The English heraldic system allows nine colours. There are two variant forms. The first recognizes two metals, five tinctures and two furs, whilst the second replaces the furs with two further tinctures. (Sometimes, confusingly, the word tincture is used as a general term to describe all heraldic colours. Here, I use the word in its strict meaning.)

The two heraldic metals are Or (gold) and Argent (silver). For practical purposes of painting, yellow and white are generally used, though in royal churches such as King's College Chapel, real gold and silver leaf were the materials applied to Or and Argent parts. The five tinctures are Azure (blue), Gules (red), Sable (black), Vert (green) and Purpure (purple). The two furs are Ermine and Vair, imitating the pelts of the stoat in wintertime, and the blue-grey squirrel, respectively.

According to Aristotelian precepts, the metals and tinctures signify the planetary spheres of pre-Copernican cosmology. Thus Or is the Sun; Argent, the Moon; Sable, Saturn; Azure, Jupiter; Gules, Mars; Vert, Venus, and Purpure, Mercury. The alternative tincture scheme, also ninefold, omitted the two furs, Vair and Sable, and substituted two new tinctures, Tenné (tawney) and Sanguine or Murrey (blood-red). The exact tint of Sanguine is described as mid-way between Gules and Purpure. The colour known as tawney was later re-named orange in popular usage.

The manuscript *Enseignement Notables aux poursuivants* in the College of Arms relates the heraldic colours to the Christian heavenly hierarchy, the members of which possess particular characteristics, which are expressed in the terms of medieval military prowess. Thus, the silvery Argent Seraphim are 'full doughty and glorious'. The 'unfaint and durable' Cherubim correspond with the dark Sable. Then come the Thrones who are 'wise and virtuous in working', with the loyal colour Azure. Next come the Principalities, who are 'hot of courage', corresponding with the ruddy Gules. The Dominations, whose colour is the blood-red Sanguine, are 'mighty of power', while the Tawney-coloured Powers are 'fortunate of victory'. The Virtues are 'knightly of government', bearing the rich royal colour purple, while the Archangels, whose verdant colour is Vert are 'keen and hardy in battle'. Finally, the angels, who are classified as 'sure messengers', correspond with the noble colour Or (gold).

According to Dame Juliana Berners, the seven planetary gems are related to the heraldic metals and tinctures: Or is topaz; Argent, pearl; Sable, diamond; Gules, ruby; Azure, sapphire; Vert, emerald, and Purpure, amethyst. English heraldry ascribes special names for jewel-like roundels in each of the nine colours. Golden roundels are called Bezant; those of silver, Plate; and red, Torteaux. Blue roundels are Hurts; black, Pellet; green, Pomeis, and purple, Golpe. The final two,

King's College Chapel, side chapel vault, painted centre

tawney and sanguine, are called Orange and Guzes respectively. The name of the colour tawney declined in use as the round citrus fruit called oranges became widely available in England. Now the colour itself is called orange, and the former name is recalled in contemporary language only by the tawny owl.

Enseignement Notables aux poursuivants lists the colours' symbolic meaning. Thus the first colour, Azure, signifies loyalty, and the sanguine humour; the second, Gules, valiant action, fire and the choleric temperament. Sable, the third colour, represents the Devil and the Earth, and in man, the melancholic humour; Sinable (green), the plants and trees, and in a man, love and courtesy. Purpure indicates riches, abundance and largesse. The first metal, Or, is the golden sun and noble goodwill in a man, whilst the second, Argent, signifies water, humility and the phlegmatic temperament.

The heraldic colours have almost limitless correspondences. Those most commonly used in medieval English tournaments, recorded in Sir John Ferne's *The Blazon of Gentrie* (1586), correspond with particular numbers and human age-groups. Azure (blue) corresponds with the planet Jupiter, the metal tin and the weekday Thursday; the virtues of justice and loyalty, or purity; the zodiacal signs of Taurus and Libra; the month of September; the blue lily; the element of air; the season of spring; the sanguine humour; the numbers four and nine, and, in the Ages of Man, boyhood (seven to fourteen years). Gules (red or vermilion) corresponds with Mars, iron and Tuesday; charity and magnanimity, or power; Aries and Cancer; March, June and July; the Gillyflower; fire; summer; choler; three and ten, and virility (thirty to forty years of age).

Sable (black) has Saturn as its planet and Saturday as its day, prudence and constancy as its virtues. Its corresponding metal is lead. The Sable zodiac signs are Capricorn and Aquarius, with December and January its months. Its flower is the Aubifaine, its element earth, and its season, winter. The black humour is melancholy, its age decrepit or crooked old age, and its numbers five and eight. Vert or Sinable is the coppery planet Venus and Friday; love, loyalty, affability and courtesy; Gemini and Virgo; August; all kinds of green plants; spring; water; the number six and lusty green youth (twenty to thirty years of age). The green temperament is phlegmatic.

Purpure corresponds with the planet Mercury, the metal quicksilver and Wednesday. The purple virtues are temperance and prudence, its zodiacal signs, Sagittarius and Pisces. The violet is the Purpure flower. Elementally, it corresponds with water and earth, whilst its season is winter. It partakes of the choleric humour, and signifies the age of grey hairs in human life. It rules the numbers seven and twelve.

King's College Chapel, angel with the arms of East Anglia

Or (gold or yellow) signifies the Sun and Sunday, the metal gold, the virtue of faith and constancy, the zodiac sign Leo, the month of July, the Marigold flower, the element of air, the season of summer, the sanguine humour, the numbers one, two and three and, in the ages of man, the young age of adolescence (fourteen to twenty years). Argent (silver or white) signifies the Moon, silver and Monday; hope and innocence, or alternatively, joy; Scorpio and Pisces; October and November; the white rose and lily flowers; autumn; the phlegmatic humour; the numbers ten and eleven, and human infancy, the first seven years of life.

By means of these colours, medieval heraldic artists expressed particular qualities that others schooled in the language could recognize immediately. It is certain that the designers of medieval churches used this Aristotelian-Christian symbolic system in choosing the appropriate colours for various parts of the building. King's College Chapel would have been one of the finest examples of this symbolism. Today, the unpainted interior is seen as the authentic expression of the chapel. Unless there is a revolutionary change in aesthetic appreciation, the painting and gilding will never be carried out, even five hundred years after the chapel's completion.

Chapter 5

The Almost-Sainted King and Glazing the Chapel

The Unauthorized Saint

King Henry VII desired the Church to canonize King Henry VI. Although several kings of pre-conquest England had become saints (Ethelbert of Kent; Ethelbert and Edmund of East Anglia; Oswald of Northumbria; Edward, King and Martyr), no post-conquest king had been made into a saint. France had St Louis, and, the argument went, 'why should not England receive the like favour, being no less beneficial to the Church of Rome?' The fact that King Henry had been deposed was deemed no hindrance to canonization, 'for God's best servants often suffer the worst afflictions'. Henry VII seems to have believed that Henry VI had prophesied his elevation to the throne, with the story that when the civil wars between Lancaster and York first began, Henry VI, seeing the young future Henry VII, remarked to his courtiers: 'See this youth will one day quietly enjoy what we at this time so much fight about.' This prophetic claim echoes the story told about Henry V.

Fuller claims that this 'made the King with much importunity to tender this his request unto the Pope. A request the more reasonable, because it was well nigh forty years since the death of that Henry, so that only the skeletons of his virtues remained in men's memories, the flesh and corruption (as one may say) of his faults being quite consumed and for gotten'.

Instead of allowing Henry VI to be canonized, Pope Alexander told Henry VII that it was not by other men's judgments of merit that a man became a saint, but only within the Pope's remit to judge men's merits. Secondly, the Pope thought that no new saints should be made, unless there were good reasons for it, for making too many saints devalues the really worthy ones. Thirdly, that the life of anyone canonized must have been exemplarily holy, by the testimony of credible witnesses. Fourthly, that credible witness must assert the truth of real miracles wrought by him after his death. Fifthly, that, even when all of these criteria had been met, the making of a saint was very expensive.

Henry VII and those who had known the king and witnessed miracles at his tomb asserted that Henry VI had indeed led an exemplary life of holiness, being unusually moral for a medieval king by professing and practising pacifism. Furthermore, by being murdered in prison, he could well be called a martyr. But the bottom line was that the Pope wanted 1,500 ducats of gold for making Henry VI a saint. The miserly English king refused to pay this service charge, and so Henry's canonization was deferred. When Pope Alexander VI died in 1503, another attempt was made with his effective successor, Julius II, but large sums of money were demanded once more. (Pius III had only lived for a few days after being elected pope in October 1503, so he had no chance to do anything effective, certainly not demand money from the king of England).

So Henry VI was never elevated to the Catholic company of saints. Not long afterwards, the break came with the Church of Rome, and the idea that there should be saints at all was rejected by many Protestants. The Archbishop of Canterbury never awarded himself the power to canonize anyone, and so it remains. Later Protestant cynics had the view that 'there was plenty of Popish Saints beside him, wherewith the Calendar is so overstocked, that for want of room they jostle one another.'

In his *A Brief Account of Westminster Abbey* (1894), W.J. Loftie wrote how King Henry VII intended the body of Henry VI to be reburied in his new chapel at Westminster. 'In his will Henry (VII) gave very careful and special directions concerning his burial, and intended that the body of Henry VI should also be laid in the new chapel. In a council held at Greenwich the rival claims of Chertsey, where he was first buried, Windsor, where he then lay, and Westminster, where he had selected a place for his tomb, were considered, and Westminster was chosen. The Abbot was charged £500, equal to at least as many thousands now, and seems actually to have paid it. He probably never saw the money again, but neither did he obtain the body of Henry VI. There seems to be no doubt that it still rests at Windsor; at all events, it was never removed to Westminster, and the

King's College Chapel, sculpture of King Henry

scanty respect shown to monuments and memorials under the Tudors and during the Civil War obliterated any marks by which his grave at Windsor could be identified.'

The Chapel Windows

If a pope had made King Henry VI a saint, doubtless episodes from his life and miracles would have become an important element in the stained glass of the chapel. But unfortunately that did not happen and the glass, though remarkable, does not have an image of Henry. Leaded painted glass had already been installed in some of the windows in the 1480s during the reign of King Richard III before the chapel's stonework was finished. But it was removed or destroyed before the end of 1515. Once the stonework was completed in that year, re-glazing commenced. This is recorded in a memorandum dated the 30th November 1515, authorizing a payment of £100 by way of imprest to Barnard Floure, the king's glazier, by Thomas Lark, the surveyor, the 'form and condition' of the work being determined by Richard Foxe, Bishop of Winchester, one of Henry VII's executors. Floure was described as 'Almain' (German). He had been appointed royal glazier in 1505, much to the annoyance of the English glaziers. He finished only the tracery glass and four of the great windows before his death, which was before the 14th of August 1517. From 1513 to 1516, Floure glazed the Savoy Hospital in London, using glass imported from the Rhineland.

After Floure died, nothing more was done for nine years. Then, on the 30th of April and the 3rd of May 1526, two contracts were placed to glaze the remaining twenty-two great windows. Galyon Hone, who came from the Low Countries, was appointed as royal glazier soon after the death of Floure. He was contracted to work on the chapel, which he did from 1526 to 1531. Subsequently, Hone made windows for Whitehall Palace, Hampton Court and Windsor Castle. Two Londoners, Richard Bond and Thomas Reve, together with

James Nicholson, another foreigner like Floure and Hone, from the Flemish-Dutch-German craftsmen's quarter at Southwark, assisted him at Cambridge. In 1518, Nicholson glazed Great St. Mary's church in Cambridge, which was then undergoing reconstruction, but none of his glass remains. He worked on the chapel from 1526 to 1528, and then worked for Cardinal Wolsey at Oxford and elsewhere. About 1530, Nicholson gave up painting glass because of its supposed idolotrous nature, and became a printer, publishing three editions of the Bible and New Testament, and several books that the orthodox considered to tend towards heresy.

Another craftsman from the Southwark colony was Francis Williamson, who worked in partnership with Symond Symondes, who had previously, in 1509, worked in Cambridge on the glazing of Christ's College. Christ's had been founded as the result of God's House being expelled from the site of King's in 1446, transferred by its founder William Bingham to St. Andrew's Street, and granted a charter by Henry VII in 1505 for expansion under the aegis of Lady Margaret Beaufort. Symondes also glazed his own parish church, St. Margaret's, Westminster, which stands to the north of Westminster Abbey inside the abbey precinct. All these glaziers had their workshops at either Southwark or London, most being craftsmen from mainland Europe working in the style of the Southwark School of glass-painting. The glaziers carried out the patterns of the designer, who, in most cases, was Dirick Vellert of Antwerp in Flanders. Vellert never came to England – his designs were sent across to the glaziers. The designs themselves bear a close resemblance to the windows, by Bernard von Orley, in St. Gudule's Cathedral in Brussels. They illustrate emblematical episodes from scripture. Most of them follow the type and ante-type principle: scenes from the Old Testament or Apocrypha are shown as precursors of episodes from the life of Christ from the New Testament and The Gospel of Nicodemus.

Travelling round the chapel, starting on the west end at the south side, the designer and glazier of each window were as follows: 1 unknown/Williamson and Symondes; 2 unknown/unknown; 3-7 Vellert/Hone; 8-11 Vellert/Reve; 12 Vellert/Reve (lower half, also originally upper half, replaced by Hedgeland 1845); 13 Vellert/Hone; 14 Vellert/Bond; 15 Vellert/Reve; 16 Vellert/Hone (upper)/unknown (lower); 17 Vellert/Hone, Coeke/Reve, unknown; 18 Vellert/Reve; 19 unknown/Nicholson; 20 Vellert/Reve; 21 unknown/ Nicholson; 22 Vellert/Hone; 23 unknown/Williamson and

King's College Chapel, glass detail

Symondes; 24 Floure designer and glazier; 25 unknown/ Williamson and Symondes.

The twelfth window in the chapel was planned to have a building, part of the great court, abutting onto it. The partially-built construction was torn down in 1827 when William Wilkins' so-called 'neo-gothic' plan for completing the court was under way. This fragment of building was all that was finished of the founder's original court, and the window was

King's College Chapel glass, Daniel in the lions' den

rebuilt to conform to the others. It was glazed by Hedgeland, of whom more later.

The finance for the window-glass came from a Praemunire (church fine) incurred by the one-time Bishop of Norwich, Richard Nix, who died in 1536. Nix, who had gone blind,

King's College Chapel glass, Elijah in the chariot of fire

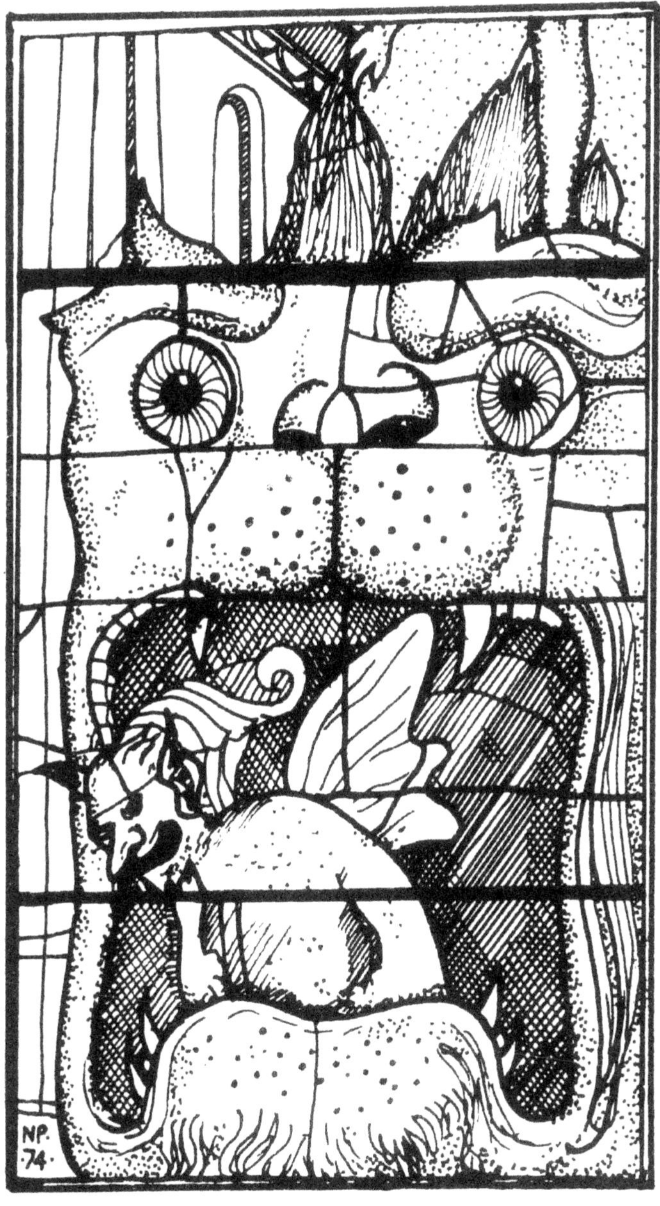

King's College Chapel glass, the mouth of Hell

having been what is described as a 'persecutor', was fined the vast sum of £10,000 for illegally extending his jurisdiction over the Mayor of Thetford.

It is notable that the layout of the windows is identical to the mnemonic diagram in Robert Fludd's (1574–1637) *Technical History of the Microcosm*, in the section 'Ars Memoria' (the art of memory). At King's College, the layout is as follows: the central panel bears the four 'messengers', figures bearing scrolls upon which are painted quotations from relevant passages in the Bible and Apocrypha. There are 94 messengers in all. Some are repeats, being drawn from only 42 cartoons. The great east window does not have messengers, and the messengers' panels are omitted from the following list.

The subjects of the windows are as follows:

Window 1: a. The translation of Enoch; b. Solomon receives his mother, Bath-Sheba; c. Assumption of the Blessed Virgin Mary; d. Coronation of the Blessed Virgin Mary.

Window 2: a. The death of Tobit; b. The burial of Jacob; c. The death of the Virgin Mary; d. Her burial.

Window 3: a. St Paul exorcizing the woman with the spirit of divination; b. Paul before the Chief Captain Lysias at Jerusalem; c. Paul's farewell at Philippi (or Miletus); d. Paul before the Emperor Nero.

Window 4: a. Conversion of Saul; b. St Paul conversing with disciples at Damascus; c. Paul and Barnabas at Lystra. The priest brings oxen to sacrifice before them; d. St Paul stoned at Lystra.

Window 5: a. St Peter and St John heal the disabled man at the Temple; b. The arrest of the Apostles; c. St Peter and the Apostles going to the Temple, the background shows Peter preaching inside it; d. Death of Ananias.

Window 6: a. Elijah transported heavenward in a chariot of fire; b. Moses receiving the Tables of the Law from the hand of God on Mount Sinai; c. The ascension of Christ; d. The descent of the Holy Spirit.

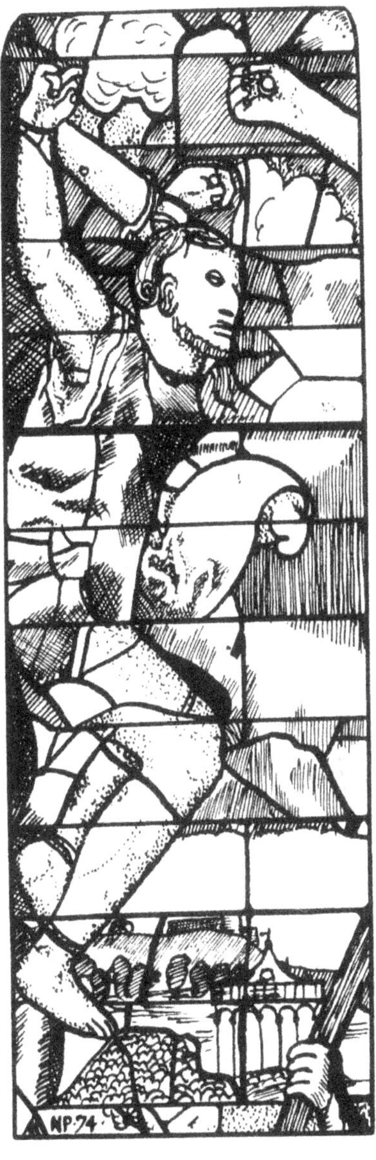

King's College Chapel
glass, crucified thief

Window 7: a. The return of the prodigal son; b. The meeting of Jacob and Joseph in Egypt; c. The unbelief of the doubting Thomas; d. Christ appearing to all the Apostles except Thomas.

Window 8: a. The angel Raphael, in the form of a young man, meets Tobias; b. Habakuk feeding Daniel in the lions' den; c. Christ, disguised as a traveller, meets the two disciples going to Emmaus; d. The supper at Emmaus, Christ recognized by the ceremony of breaking the bread.

Window 9: a. Reuben finds the pit empty and Joseph gone; b. Darius visits the lions' den, and finds Daniel alive; c. The three Marys discover Christ's empty tomb; d. Christ, holding a spade, appears to Mary Magdalene in the garden.

Window 10: a. Jonah regurgitated by the whale; b. Anna, the mother of Tobias, who had given him up for dead, sees him return alive with Azarius; c. The resurrection of Christ; d. Christ appearing to his mother at prayer.

Window 11: a. Joseph cast into the pit by his brothers; b. The Israelites going out of Egypt, Pharaoh's army drowning in the Red Sea; c. The burial of Christ; d. The harrowing of Hell: Christ overcoming Death and the Devil.

Window 12: The upper half (a and b) is not part of the sixteenth century schema. It dates from the nineteenth century; c. Naomi and her daughters-in-law lament Elimelech, her husband; d. The Virgin and other holy women lamenting over the dead Christ.

Window 13: The east window. Tracery: in the centre, the arms of King Henry VII on a banner held by a red dragon; in the side-lights, the red rose of Lancaster, and the red-and-white Tudor Rose, the feather of the Prince of Wales with a scroll bearing his motto 'Ich Dien' (I serve), the fleur-de-lys and the initials HR, HE and HK. Ich Dien, one of the two mottoes of the Black Prince, has been used by all Princes of Wales ever since. In this window, the mnemonic layout is not used. There are no messengers with inscriptions, and in the first three lights below the transom is the *Ecce Homo* (behold the Man). In the centre three, Pontius Pilate is washing his hands. In the centre, Christ is represented with His back to the spectator. In the three on the right, Christ is shown, bearing the cross, with Saint Veronica offering her napkin to wipe His face. Legend tells how it then took on the image of Christ's face, and now is one of the four great relics preserved in the piers of the dome at St. Peter's at Rome. Above the transom, the left three lights contain the nailing to the cross. In the centre, Christ is shown crucified between the two thieves. In the right three lights, Christ's body is taken down from the cross.

Window 14: a. Three demons tormenting Job; b. The coronation of Solomon; c. The scourging of Christ; d. Christ crowned with thorns.

Window 15: a. Jeremiah in prison; b. Noah mocked by Ham; c. Christ before Annas; d. Christ before Herod.

Window 16: a. Cain murders Abel; b. Shemei curses King David; c. The Kiss of Judas. Peter attacks Malchus, who has on his left arm the name NALCKEN; d. Christ blindfolded and mocked.

Window 17: a. The fall of manna; b. The fall of the Rebel Angels; c. The Last Supper; d. Christ's agony in the garden. The Holy Grail is shown at the left upper corner.

Window 18: a. Elisha raises the Shunammite's son; b. The triumph of King David; c. The raising of Lazarus; d. The entry of Christ into Jerusalem.

Window 19: a. Naaman the leper washing himself in the Jordan; b. Jacob tempts Esau to sell his birthright; c. Christ's baptism in the River Jordan; d. The temptation of Christ.

Window 20: a. The Golden Calf standing on a pillar of ruby, being worshipped by the Jews. Moses casts down the Tables of the Law. On them is the Flemish inscription, 'DUS ELSTE LIEF GODT BOVE ALEN' (Thou shalt love God above all); b. The massacre of the Seed Royal by Athaliah; d. The images of the Egyptian gods are cast down. At the bottom is the number 15017, read by some as the date 1517; d. The massacre of the innocents.

Window 21: a. The purification of women under the law; b. Jacob's flight from Esau; c. The presentation of Christ in the Temple; d. The flight into Egypt.

Window 22: a. The circumcision of Isaac by Abraham; b. The visit of the Queen of Sheba to Solomon; c. The circumcision of Christ; d. The adoration of the Magi.

Window 23: a. The temptation of Eve; b. Moses and the burning bush; c. The annunciation; d. The nativity.

Window 24: a. The Presentation of the golden table in the Temple of the Sun. Valerius Maximus tells the story as follows: 'Someone had purchased the produce of their next cast from some fishermen who were drawing their nets near Miletus. They brought up a great golden Delphic table (or tripod) and a dispute arose; they said they had sold their catch of fish, the other asserted that he had bought whatever the cast might bring up. It was agreed to consult the oracle of Apollo at Delphi, who said: "He who is the first of all men in wisdom, to him let the tripod be given." So they offered it to Thales of Miletus. He, in modesty yielded it to Bias of Prione, and he to Pittacus: thus it went the round of the Seven Wise Men of Greece, till it reached Solon of Athens who, judging the god to be the wisest, offered the prize to Apollo'. There is an image of the god on a pedestal. This is taken to be a type of b. The presentation of the Virgin in the Temple; c. The Marriage of Tobias and Sara; d. The Marriage of Joseph and Mary.

Window 25: a. The offering of Joachim and Anna is rejected by the High Priest; b. Joachim is bidden by the angel to go to Jerusalem, where he will meet his wife at the Golden Gate of the Temple; c. Joachim and Anna at the Golden Gate; d. Anna gives birth to the Virgin Mary.

Window 26: The Last Judgement, showing Christ, the Apostles and Saints above, with the saved on the left and the damned on the right beneath them.

Maintenance and Restoration

Glass in lead requires periodic maintenance. The lead cames (or calms) that hold the glass in place, though sturdy, gradually weaken through continued expansion and contraction and oxidation. Cement falls out, rain penetrates, and the iron saddle-bars become subject to rust. Sometimes, birds collide with windows and crack or break the glass. Hailstorms and human activity can also break them. So the windows of King's College Chapel have been repaired and re-leaded (with new lead cames) on a number of occasions. They were repaired in 1570-71, 1591-92 and 1616-17. They were re-leaded and had their saddle-bars renewed in 1657-59. Further repairs were needed in 1711-12, 1720-21 and 1725-30, when a glazier called Belcher was paid £523 for the work. In 1757-65, at the cost of £1,600, the stonework of the reveals and mullions was renewed, and the windows were again patched and re-leaded. Between 1842 and 1849, at a cost of £200 per window, J.P. Hedgeland patched and re-leaded and repainted or replaced a considerable portion of the glass. This involved at least one new head on a figure, and the obliteration of scrolls and other features. In *The Guardian* (No. 7, 21st November 1849), a protest over 'this work of destruction' finally succeeded in bringing Hedgeland's over-zealous restoration to a halt. Between 1893 and 1906, those windows that were untouched by Hedgeland's heavy hand were restored as far as was possible by C.E. Kempe. During World War II, all the glass except the tracery was removed to an underground bunker for safe keeping. It was cleaned, repaired, re-leaded and photographed before it was put back, six years after the end of the war, in 1951.

Chapter 6

Internal Fittings, the Chantries and Alterations

The Fittings in Their Historical Context

The west window was glazed with plain glass, as money for stained glass had run out on Archbishop Fisher's imprisonment for opposing Henry VIII's divorce (October 1530). Only in the years 1878–79 was it finally glazed with coloured glass by the company of Clayton and Bell, with the theme of the Last Judgement. In the early 1530s, once most of the painted glass was in the windows, the next job was installing the interior fittings. At this point, the original Perpendicular architecture was abandoned, and a wooden screen in the Renaissance style was made and erected by foreign craftsmen, probably Italian, between June 1533 and May 1536. A high altar, carved with images by Magistro Antonio, was delivered in 1554–55.

The screen is as wide, and in the same position, as the stone one stipulated by the founder. The money for it was provided by Henry VIII after a petition from the college to complete a great deal of the outstanding work. This included the high altar and sixteen others, of stone; the entire paving; the screen; the metal fittings; stalls; doors; images and painting and gilding the main vault. To fit the wooden screen, some of the heraldic stonework was smashed. The cost was estimated at £2,893. The oaken stalls, also Renaissance in style, date from between 1536 and 1538.

During this tumultuous period in England's affairs, Protestant tracts were being exported directly from north Germany to Cambridge, where they had a ready audience in the university. A sect of Protestants known simply as the Germans met at the White Horse Inn in the town. The Catholic faith was now under threat, with the foundation of the Church of

England and the beginning of sectarian persecutions. In 1535, Cambridge's religious guild of Corpus Christi was suspended. Later restored by the Catholic queen, Mary, it was finally suppressed by Queen Elizabeth I. The canopy covering the Host took fire during the final procession of the Guild, and this was held to be an ill omen.

In 1538, the dissolution of the monasteries began, and, in 1545, an Act for the dissolution of the universities was drawn up. However, it was not put into effect. The members of King's College, with a tempting revenue of £1,010 *per annum*, appealed to Katharine Parr to intercede with the king, which she did successfully. Although Henry VIII destroyed the monasteries, most of the monastic hospitals and the almshouses, thereby obliterating what inadequate welfare system there was for the sick, poor and old, the two universities were spared the same fate. At this time, sectarianism

King's College Chapel,
west window exterior

became so vicious that John Frith and Laurence Sanders were burnt alive publicly for religious offences, as were Robert Glover and John Hullier, the latter killed on Jesus Green during Mary's reign just for writing a tract on the Common-Prayer. All were from King's College.

The chapel was just about finished, when the religious observance for which it was built was destroyed. Its opening, when the old chapel collapsed, was at the time of the dissolution. The purpose had changed, but the building remained, its innate numerology, geometry and symbolism remaining as testimony to its true purpose as an instrument of enlightenment.

Alterations and Changes

The subsequent history of the chapel is one of constant alteration and change, taking it progressively further from the founder's intention. For some reason, the original doors were removed early in the seventeenth century. The present north, south and west doors were made in 1614–15 by Henry Man. At the same time, Jacobean images of palm trees, cherubim and the tetragrammaton (the four-character Hebrew name of God, JHVH) were carved in the tympanum at the west end. Although in a style not in keeping with the medieval west end, the symbolic carving did express the esoteric significance of the building.

An organ was not installed in the chapel until 1606 (by Dallam). It was taken down, and the pipes sold, by order of Parliament during Cromwell's Commonwealth. The present organ was built in 1688 by Rene Harris, but has suffered at least three reconstructions since then. Fortunately, the windows survived the puritanical zeal of William Dowsing, the Cromwellian church wrecker, possibly through the appointment of Dr Whitchcot as Provost of King's College by the Long Parliament. Legend has it that Dowsing accepted a bribe of 6s 8d from the Dean to spare the windows. This is unlikely, as religious mania, not personal aggrandisement, was the drive of the fanatic Dowsing. Another legend is the totally impossible claim that all of the windows were taken out in one night by a man and a boy, and buried before Dowsing arrived with his hammer. In fact, only a few easily accessible carvings suffered the hammer blow of iconoclasm.

The Chantries

King's College Chapel proper has eighteen side-chapels, some of which were once used as chantries. Until their suppression during the Reformation, chantries were private tomb-chapels, each endowed by an individual in order that masses might be sung until the Last Judgement for the health of the soul of the departed in Purgatory. Fine chapels were built, often in the form of miniature buildings, in which the dead person was buried, and where the services were held for the soul. At King's they are not in the form of many chantries in cathedrals, which take the form of small self-contained buildings within the main body of the building.

King's College Chapel south side, east end

These side-chapels occupy the spaces formed between ten of the eleven buttresses on the northern and southern side of the chapel proper. They have the main plinth of the chapel continued across their external faces, horizontal cornices carved with portcullises, Tudor roses, fleur-de-lys and foliated paterae, and pierced parapet walls. These pierced parapet walls are continued at a higher level over the north and south doors. The side-chapel walls are composed mainly of broad eight-light windows. On each side of the chapel proper, the upper portions of the windows have, in all, thirteen curvilinear panels and five rectilinear.

Henry VI's original scheme intended fewer side chapels than were finally constructed. The departure from the Will of the Founder is that it envisaged only those connected to the ante-chapel, and a two storey vestry measuring fifty by twenty-two feet, divided into two rooms on each floor north of the choir (ie. the side of old court, and next to the old chapel). This is one of the few departures from the original plan, providing what later became chantries for departed King's College officials. The practice of endowing chantries

King's College Chapel south side, exterior middle

was suppressed at the Reformation, and plays no part in Protestant ritual.

On the south side of the main chapel, the second small chapel from the west, was the chantry of Robert Hacomblen, D.D. Hacomblen was provost when some of the great windows were erected, he wrote *Comments on Aristotle's Ethicks*, and he donated the magnificent brass lectern which now stands in the choir. In the glass of this chapel are the evangelistic symbols and the four fathers of the Latin Church; St. Jerome, St. Ambrose, St. Augustine and St. Gregory. Hacomblen's monumental brass depicts him dressed in surplice and almuce with a scroll coming from his mouth with an inscription in blackletter characters upon it. The figure is surrounded by a marginal inscription-fillet bearing the four symbols of the evangelists, one at each corner, and a shield showing the five wounds of Christ that retain traces of red enamel.

The chapel immediately to the east of Hacomblen's Chantry is Provost Brassie's Chapel, where he was buried in 1558 (he was provost from 1556 to 1558). Robert Brassie, S.T.P. is depicted on his memorial brass dressed in surplice, almuce and stole. The brass shows traces of an inlay of white metal. Below the figure is a plate with a blackletter inscription in Latin which, translated, reads 'Here lies Robert Brassie, Doctor of Divinity, formerly Provost of this College, who departed this life 10th November, A.D. 1558'. Two shields, and a scroll emanating from the mouth, have been destroyed by iconoclasts. This is strange, because Brassie's chapel dates from Protestant times.

The easternmost chantry on the south side was dedicated to John Argentine, who was provost from 1501 to 1507. In this chapel is another monumental brass. This shows the figure of a man in academic dress, with an inscription on a scroll coming from his mouth. Below the effigy is an inscription-plate. On the scroll is a Latin supplication, which, translated, reads: 'O Christ, Son of the Virgin, Crucified Lord, Redeemer of Mankind, remember me'. On the inscription plate are the words (again in Latin): 'This stone buries the body of John Argentine, Master of Arts, Physician, Preacher of the Gospel; Passenger, remember, thou art mortal, pray in a humble posture, that my soul may live in Christ, in a state of immortality'. On a fillet around the stone upon which brasses are mounted is written (also in Latin): 'Pray for the soul of John Argentine, Master of Arts, doctor of physic and divinity, and Provost of this college, who died 2nd February, 1507, May God have mercy on his soul. Amen'. In the corners of the fillet were the four evangelists' symbols. Those of St. Mark and St. Matthew are missing, but the other two retain traces of red enamel. There were also four heraldic escutcheons, three of which are still extant with the arms of Argentine. A scroll and crucifixion have been destroyed deliberately by puritan fanatics.

In 1920-21, this chantry was converted into a war memorial chapel to commemorate those members of the college who perished in the Great War of 1914-19. Then it was re-named the All Souls Chapel.

On the north side of the building, the second small side chapel from the east is the chantry dedicated to William Towne. This was the first part of the building to be roofed, in 1461. Towne's chantry commemorates William Towne, D.D., who was a Fellow of King's. It contains the oldest monumental brass in the chapel. This consists of an effigy of a man in academic dress holding a scroll (defaced) in Gothic writing. Below is a plate with a Latin inscription (the supplication also partially defaced by Puritan zealots): 'Pray for the soul of master William Towne, Doctor of Divinity, once a Fellow of this College, who died on the eleventh day of March 1494. Whose soul God Pardon. Amen.'

The side-chapel second from the west on the north side was fitted out as a memorial to the founder in 1930–32. The windows of the side-chapels are filled with a multiplicity of fragments of painted glass, mostly of medieval date. In the first chapel from the east on the northern side, there are beautiful fragments unearthed when the Old Cavendish Laboratories were built, on the site of Cambridge's Augustinian Priory. Remnants of the original glass in the first three chapels from the east on the north side show that originally there were at least ten apostles and eight prophets represented. In the second chapel from the east are stained glass panels which were originally in the old east range of the schools, removed in 1748, and obtained by an exchange of glass with the church at Greenford, Middlesex. The fourth chapel from the east on this side has glass with the scratched craftsmen's inscriptions: 'Thos. Stevens Glazier 1761' and 'James Mills, Glazier and Plumber, cleaned these windows John Leach Feb. 1806'. In the next side-chapel westward is the scratching 'John Hennebert Plumber and Glazier 1767'. In the second from westernmost on the north side, amongst many other pieces, are two quarries with windmills, inscribed 'As God will 1557'. The window of the westernmost side chapel on the north is composed in the main of glass dating from 1850, other than the coat of arms of Benjamin Whichcote, Provost 1644-60, signed and dated by John Clarke, 1650. This, however, was inserted in 1924.

On the southern side, the easternmost chantry, that of Argentine, the windows contain an early sixteenth century Flemish or Rhenish glass, which was, however, inserted in 1920. Another part of the window has a figure of God the Father, originally from La Chenu church, north of Tours in France. Flemish glass can be found in the next chapel, but again, although authentic, it was bought from St. Catherine's college in 1921. In the third chapel from the west on the south side there is much original glass, heavily restored in 1857 by Constable. One quarry is inscribed with the name of Robert Brassie. In the next chapel west, the majority of glass is also by

Constable, excepting the images of the four founders of the Latin Church, which date from around 1520. The scratching 'John Barker 1744 Glazier and Plumber' can also be detected. The last side-chapel has glass which bears the arms of Martin Freeman, Fellow of King's, who died in 1630.

King's College Chapel, east window

The fragmentary nature of the side-chapel windows, with their consequent lack of original glass, is a reminder of an iconoclastic past and savage 'restorations', as the artistic vandalism of the eighteenth, nineteenth and twentieth centuries were called. Between 1920 and 1930, by installing old glass culled from many sources, the amount of painted glass was increased from twenty lights in five chapels to fifty-seven in nine chapels, excluding the tracery lights, much of which are original.

The side-chapels are, in general, floored with square red tiles, though there are two examples of mid-fourteenth century incised tiles, possibly originating in the earlier church on the site, St. John's Zachary. Two others are of smashed stone slabs. The side-chapels are roofed with lead. On the roof of the fourth chapel from the west on the north side is an inscription cast in lead sheeting, recording the re-leading of 'these small chapels' in 1829 by I. Greef, Plumber.

The Much-Altered East End

The east end of any church is the most sacred part. Often called 'the sanctuary', it is the place where the high altar stands, where the priest conducts the most sacred rites and ceremonies of his religion. The east end of King's College Chapel was never finished in the manner intended, owing to the advent of Protestantism. This led to the interior of the eastern end being panelled in the seventeenth century. In 1633, Thomas Weaver gave the chapel carved oaken panelling with armorial bearings. Canopies were made between 1675 and 1678 by Cornelius Austin at the cost of £305. In 1678-79 Austin added the panelling over the north and south doors further east.

This fine seventeenth century panelling was torn out in the mid-1960s as part of the so-called 'liturgical renewal' fashionable at the time. This act of destruction revealed a considerable amount of sixteenth century inscriptions on the original stones. They were made in ochre and charcoal. One showed a horse, another the date 29th April 1524, and others, semi-legible handwriting. Much of this contemporary evidence was deliberately scrubbed off after the panelling was removed, and it is now very faint. The oak pulpit, hexagonal with four linen-fold panels in each face in moulded panelling, open below and with its corner styles continued to form legs, is now in the church of St. Edward, King and Martyr, down St Edward's Passage opposite the entrance to King's College.

The arrangements and fittings of the east end have been changed and modified on numerous occasions, for both religious and aesthetic reasons. In the reign of Queen Elizabeth I, who attended two services and a performance of the play *Aulularia* by Plautus in the chapel on the same Sunday, the Renaissance style high altar was ripped out and destroyed. As the foundation stone was below the point where the original high altar, and perhaps the relics, stood (there were relics in the first chapel), so it is probable that the foundation stone was removed at the same time that the high altar was demolished. We will never know, because the remains of the altar platform in which it was located were summarily destroyed in the 1960s to accommodate the Rubens painting of *The Adoration of the Magi.*

In 1633 and 1634, Woodroffe built a screen across the east end, forming a reredos, the Church of England communion table being set against it and railed about. Panelling by Cornelius Austin was installed at the east end in 1662-63. In the eighteenth century, a totally new arrangement was designed by James Essex, who searched for the foundation stone without success. With stonework by Jeffs and Bentley and woodwork by Charles Humfrey, Sr. and Cotton, the new layout was begun in 1770, and finished in 1776 at the cost of £1,652. James Essex was the architect of the old 1782 Guildhall of Cambridge, 1782, now demolished.

During the nineteenth century, more alterations were undertaken. In his *Notes on the History and Present Condition of King's*

College Chapel, (1867) Thomas John Proctor Carter quotes a then recent report by George Gilbert Scott, R.A., for proposed alterations to the choir of King's College Chapel, which was drawn up at the request of certain fellows of the college. This involved a search for the location of the original high altar:

> Having carefully examined into the question as to where the high altar of King's College Chapel originally stood, the following are the only evidences which I can find.
>
> 1st. I have made a minute examination of the eastern wall, and can find no marks whatever against it of an altar or a reredos, or of any painting indicative of either having existed there, but the ashlar stonework runs through, smooth and clean, excepting only the coat of coloured wash, which exists there as elsewhere.
>
> 2nd. I dug down where the altar would have stood had it been against the eastern wall, but could find no signs of a foundation.
>
> 3rd. The ashlar at the east end commences at about the level of the present altar platform, which is nine inches above the present general level of the pavement of the eastern bay. The cills of the doorways leading into the stair-turrets are at the same level, and the ashlar in the side walls of the bay commences at the same level, showing distinctly that this was the original level of the pavement of this bay, that is to say, that it was nine inches higher than at present. The ashlar drops a little at the termination of the bay, and again, in a greater degree, at about six feet further to the westward, and thence it coincides in level with the present pavement.
>
> This shows that the pavement of the whole of the eastern bay was six steps, or 2 feet 4½ inches above that of the third bay, and that the steps, and, probably, a second and narrow platform occupied the eastern part of the

second bay, the remainder of it being level with the third bay.

4th. There is, I believe, no mention in the will of the founder of the position of the altar, though there is a good deal of indirect evidence in favour of its having been in advance of the eastern end, and which is corroborated by my finding no trace of its ever having existed at that end.

5th. The will of the founder, in speaking of Eton college chapel, specifically directs that the altar, with its reredos, should be placed eight feet in advance of the east wall, – from which, taken in conjunction with the evidences above stated, I conclude that the same arrangement was intended to have been carried out in King's College Chapel.

In any alteration of the altar arrangements, therefore, I would recommend a return to this – the probable idea of the founder – I would raise the whole eastern bay to the level indicated by the commencement of the ashlar; a little in advance of this bay I would drop two steps, as indicated by the drop in the ashlar level; thence I would have a platform of some four or five feet wide, with a flight of four more steps in advance of it, leading down to the present level of the second and third bays.

I would place the altar-table on a raised foot-pace, at about the centre of the eastern bay, or half a bay in advance of the east wall, thus following the rule laid down by the founder for Eton college chapel. This will necessitate a *detached* reredos, as is described for Eton, and which should be of rich materials and workmanship. I would substitute for the present rich, though not very tasteful wainscot-work which lines the eastern bay, rich hangings reaching to the window cills. If contemporary

> tapestry of suitable character could be procured, this would be the finest material for the purpose, but failing this, it would become a matter of consideration what would be the best substitute which could now be obtained; possibly something might be done on the principle recently adopted for the hangings behind the stalls in Cologne cathedral, though treated in better art.
>
> The seventeenth century linings of the second and third bays should remain. These have formerly been hung with tapestry, possibly on special occasions, but this will not now be necessary, if the eastern bay is so decorated. There should be sedilia, which had, probably, be better of wood, as there is no sign, that I have been able to discover, of stone sedilia ever having existed.
>
> I will not at present offer any suggestion as to the treatment of the reredos, but will content myself with suggesting, generally, that it must be of material and art proportioned to the magnificence of the building.
>
> **Geo. Gilbert Scot**
> **20, Spring Gardens, Charing Cross,**
> **London, S.W., January 2nd, 1866**
>
> (Since the above was written the conclusion I had arrived at has been rendered a certainty by the discovery of a notice of the position of the foundation stone of the altar in a contemporary manuscript which states it to have been traced 14 feet from the east – **G.G.S.**)

George Gilbert Scott's nineteenth century proposal attempted, as far as was possible, to follow the original intentions of the founder. Further schemes, by William Burges in 1874, and J. Pearson in 1889 were also not proceeded with. Even when they overdid their restorations, these Victorian architects had a real sympathy with medieval work, using traditionally-trained craftsmen; their painted interiors evoked the spirit of the medieval workmen. (This spirit can be experienced in the church of All Saints, Jesus Lane, by G.F. Bodley 1863-64, with interior design by William Morris and Pre-Raphaelite artists, now restored.) The architects of the 'postwar' twentieth century when 'the New Brutalism' was the vogue did not treat the medieval tradition so explicitly stated in the founder's wishes so reverently.

Thomas Garner made a new altar in 1902, and a new reredos, with Arts and Crafts communion rails and panelling made by Detmar Blow and Ferdinand Billery in 1911. All this new work survived barely half a century, as, in 1960, Robert Maguire and Keith Murray were appointed to 're-establish the high altar visually and liturgically as the focal point (sic) of the chapel'. These two had already decided to tear out the panelling of the east end as far back as the choir stalls, when, in May 1961, Major A.E. Allnatt donated a painting, *The Adoration of the Magi* by Peter Paul Rubens, to the college, and the plans underwent a major revision. Originally, Rubens had painted it as the high altarpiece for the Carmelite Convent at Leuven (Louvain) in Flanders (now Belgium). Allnatt stipulated that it must be set on the east-west axis of the chapel if the college were to accept the gift. This meant effectively that it must be set up as an altarpiece, for it would be meaningless blocking the door at the west end. As it had cost him the then enormous sum of £275,000, it was a condition that the college administration willingly agreed to.

Maguire and Murray originally intended to use the altar as what they called the 'sacrificial centrepiece', bringing it a bay and a half nearer to the congregation, with the priest celebrating holy communion in the westward-facing position, in the style of the so-called 'liturgical renewal' of the time. This 'liturgical renewal' inevitably failed to reconcile modernist Protestantism with centuries-old symbolic ritual, and it was most out of place in medieval churches designed specifically for traditional Catholic rites and ceremonies. The introduction of the compulsory Rubens *Adoration* to the plans forced the architects to carry the destruction of the sanctuary to an even greater degree than even they had intended. A new plan was evolved that involved demolishing completely the altar platform, despite the fact that this was an essential part of King Henry VI's plan.

During the revision of the plans to accommodate the Rubens, Maguire's services to the college were terminated. It seems that the college administration considered him to be not compliant enough with their wishes, and instead of him, they appointed Sir Martyn Beckett, Bart., an aristocratic architect who had worked for the National Trust on stately homes. Once the new plan had been authorized, pneumatic drills were used to demolish the remaining fifteenth century brickwork of the altar platform and steps, which had been laid 500 years earlier by pious workmen according to the principles of the

King's College Chapel, sixteenth century graffiti

spiritual arts and crafts. This was done so that the outsize Rubens would not obstruct the lower part of the east window.

Beckett's scheme was finally completed in 1968. The result was an unconvincing attempt to mix medieval Perpendicular and Renaissance art with a baroque painting and 1960s 'coffee-bar moderne' and 'brutalist minimalist' style without regard to the true purpose of the chapel as a microcosm of creation. £110,000 was spent on destroying irreplaceable features stipulated in the founder's will, so that the Rubens would look good on television when the Festival of Nine Lessons and Carols was broadcast from the chapel each Christmas Eve. It does, but the cost to the building's spirituality has been incalculable.

Chapter 7

The Altered Surroundings

The chapel is the only major building that was built according to the plans of Henry's projected college. Fuller, in his church history, writes 'The whole college was intended conformable to the chapel: but the untimely death (or rather deposing) of King Henry the Sixth hindered the same'. Stow, in his *Chronicle*, says 'I suppose that if the rest of the House had proceeded according to the chapel already finished as his (Henry VI – N.P.) full intent and meaning was, the like College could scarce have been found again in any Christian land.'

For many years, the only college buildings were the chapel and Old Court. Brick Building, south-east of the chapel, was built in the seventeenth century, and completed in 1693. It lasted until the nineteenth century. The separate timber-frame bell tower fell into disrepair and was removed in the eighteenth century. The site of the bell tower, thirty yards from the west door, appears as 'crop-patterns' in aerial photographs. Early artists' depictions of the college show a pair of bowling greens next to the river, the space between them and the chapel being exactly the size of the cloister directed by the founder, but never built. These disappeared at the laying out of King's Lawn in 1772.

Subsequent to Brick Building's completion, nothing was done to further the completion of the founder's scheme until Dr John Adams, Provost from 1712 to 1720, set up a building fund. In 1714, Toft Monk's wood, which belonged to the College, was cut down and the wood sold for £2,640, which was added to the fund. In 1713, Nicholas Hawksmoor, aided by Sir Christopher Wren, prepared plans and scale models for the completion of the college. In Hawksmoor's unique baroque style, they included a cloister and bell tower to be located at the same place as decided upon by Henry VI. This was to have been part of the grand scheme for the reconstruction of the town centre of Cambridge, the last plan to perpetuate the old market to river link of the medieval town. The funds to build this fine scheme were not forthcoming.

In 1724, the Scottish baroque architect James Gibbs was paid to draw up plans for a court measuring two hundred and forty by two hundred and eighty-two feet. In 1724, the foundation stone was laid. But of Gibbs' scheme, the only part completed was the fellows' building. This was built by Christopher Cass, citizen and mason of London. Gibbs was not paid fully until 1759. The foundation stone of Gibbs' building was the block with a saw-cut across it, which Loggan depicted as standing in the foreground of his 1688 engraving of the chapel. Folklore tells how it was being sawn by two masons when news of the death of Henry VI arrived. Packing up their tools, they left, thinking that the building would never be completed. The stone then stood in the green beside the

King's College Chapel, west end

chapel from 1461 until 1724, when it was used by Gibbs as the foundation stone.

In 1784, Robert Adam drew up a scheme for the college's completion, but to no avail. The same fate befell the neo-medieval plans of 1795 of James Wyatt. In 1823, William Wilkins produced a plan which was submitted to a committee consisting of Wilkins himself, Jeffry Wyatt and John Nash, after having won first prize in a competition for the completion. It included a plan to medievalise the classical Gibbs Building, in order to harmonize it with the chapel. Other buildings were demolished, and the Tudoresque scheme was built between 1824 and 1828. The first dinner was held in the newly-completed hall on February 27th 1828. The gate-hall of King's gatehouse continues the symbolic measures of the chapel, measuring sixteen feet by twenty-five (the squares of four and five).

The screen wall which to-day fronts on King's Parade replaced houses. At the same time, the buildings in front of the college were demolished, and railings were erected. The screen was intended to be one wall of a covered walk, never built. The iron railings were sawn off for salvage during the early part of World War II, at the same time that St John's College was erecting new ones; the date 1940 in Roman numerals can be seen on the St John's railings and gateway opposite the Holy Sepulchre church.

The college bridge over the Granta dates from 1819. It is the work of William Wilkins. It cost £3,771, replacing an older bridge, further downstream on the founder's site which had been rebuilt from the original (1472–73) bridge in 1627 by George Thompson, but was condemned as unsafe by Rennie in 1818. The fountain in the centre of the great court was designed by H.A. Armstead, and built in 1879.

The present picturesque setting of King's College Chapel dates from the eighteenth century. Hawksmoor's grand plans for straight avenues linking focal points in the manner of

Renaissance Rome were never carried out. But the university senate house was built on a site close to King's. Designed also by James Gibbs and built between 1722 and 1768, it was part of a larger scheme, unbuilt through lack of funds. Oriented due east-west, with entrances at the east and south and the ceremonial dais at the west end, the Senate House is in Gibbs' classical style, fronted by fine attached Corinthian columns. It is also notable because it is fronted by some of the earliest cast-iron railings in England. Fortunately, these did not fall to the 1940's scrapman.

Between the senate house and King's College Chapel, behind these cast-iron railings stands another part of the picturesque setting, the replica of the Warwick vase. This copy, given by Hugh, third Duke of Northumberland to Cambridge University in 1842, was made around 1830 by Sir Edward Thomason at Birmingham. It stands on a cast-iron block, which, until 1936 had a wooden casing, painted to resemble stone. It is now encased in real stone, with lettering by Eric Gill. Opposite the senate house, forming the end of King's Parade, is the nineteenth century chateau style Gonville and Caius College. This replaced vernacular houses. On the other side of the street is the medieval Great St Mary's church, used by the university for religious ceremonies. The geomantic centre of the city is marked by a disc set on the southern side of the church's west door, the traditional location for city measures and markers.

This change in the nature of the area from commerce to academe came about as a result of the university closing the river towpaths, thus preventing river traffic, which was horse-hauled on this stretch, from reaching the hithes along that part of the river. For a while, a causeway existed in the middle of the river, and the horses walked in the river pulling the barges. The town's commercial interests, suffering through the reduction in transport facilities, had a Cambridge–London canal surveyed in 1778. But it was never started. When the link to London was made, it was a railway, whose station, designed by Sancton Wood in 1845, was kept at a 'safe distance' from the university, in the distant and enclosed Middle Field.

King's College Chapel, north east view 2010

Chapter 8

Location and Orientation

Craftsmanship and True Principles

In the middle ages, the techniques and traditions of craftsmanship were taught according to the traditional guild system, through which ancient skills and wisdom were transmitted directly from master to apprentice. The creation of artefacts was in no way separated from the spiritual dimension of existence. Techniques had been developed continuously from the beginning of the respective crafts, and had come unchanged in essence through changes in prevailing religion, being based upon transcendent true principles. The sacred principles embodied in building craftsmanship were essentially the same whether employed in making temples, churches, mosques or synagogues. In medieval times, craftwork was made mindfully of God, manifesting as far as possible what was seen as His divine harmony. Whatever was created was primarily for use, instruction or delight, made with a loving and respectful spirit for the service of God and the community.

In medieval Europe, then, no church or mosque was built merely as an ornamented shed, its dimensions determined by the amount of money available, or even the size of the plot upon which it was to be built. The 'shed' way of building is the common, profane form of building in modern times, but this careless way of making is alien to the spiritual arts and crafts practised by medieval craftsmen. King's College Chapel is something different from careless modernity. It is the epitome of a sacred building. Its site was investigated for its spiritual qualities, and in its dimensions it reflected a sacred language translated into number. Number, in turn, ruled the system of proportion and linear dimensions to which the chapel was constructed.

King's College Chapel, heraldry above south entrance

Location and Sanctity

The history of King's College Chapel's location is significant. It was not just built on a piece of unoccupied land that happened to be available at the time King Henry VI decided

King's College Chapel, from The Backs

to build it. A church, a religious college and houses were demolished and the main street of a prosperous inland port was closed in order that the chapel could be built upon the precise place chosen for it. This was not an easy thing for even a king to carry out, for property had to be purchased, and a consecrated church and its churchyard removed. Naturally, there were objections to the project. The closure of a main street in order to build the college over it was the cause of a riot as late as 1454.

The church of St John's Zachary was abolished, and its Flemish curate, Nicholas Cloos, who had lost his position, was later promoted to the rank of a Bishop. The chapel's foundation stone was laid by the King in person, on an auspicious day. From the site, the projected dimensions, according to the sacred canon of proportion and measure interpreted by the King, were laid out.

As a peaceful house of God, built as an image of the cosmic order, the clerics of King's College Chapel enforced the rule that whenever a soldier entered it wearing spurs or carrying a sword, a fine was demanded from him for profaning God's peace. This is the principle of respecting a sanctuary that exists in all western religious traditions. Weapons were not allowed inside the tabernacle or the temple of the ancient Jews, inside the mosques and *haram* places of Islam, or within the *vebond* of the heathen temples of northern Europe. The prohibition at King's lapsed in the 1830s.

Orientation

In England in 1443, sacred geometry was a fine art. This ancient knowledge was taught by the monastic schools, the universities and to the apprentices of the free masons and carpenters' guilds by their masters. The most able masters of the craft guilds experimented continuously with extensions of their traditions, producing new forms with ever more sophisticated refinements. Location and orientation were elements of this geometric art of surveying. But unlike the later secularized surveying practised by civil engineers, where utilitarianism was the guiding principle, the spiritual dimension was integral with the techniques of the medieval masters.

With a few special exceptions, medieval churches and chapels in England were generally oriented east–west, with the altar at the eastern end. Traditional adherents of the Jewish, Christian and Moslem religions all orientate themselves when they pray. In prayer, Jews of the Diaspora are supposed to face Jerusalem whilst Moslems face Mecca. Ideally, synagogues and mosques are oriented towards their respective holy cities. Both are seen as the centres of their corresponding worlds. Because Christian rites and ceremonies are a complex syncretization of Jewish and ancient Pagan ideas, the Christian Churches have a less well-defined version of orientation. Some claim that orientation has a geomantic function, comparable with the Moslem praying towards the Ka'aba at Mecca. Symbolically, this means facing towards the centre of the world, which medieval Christian geographers defined as the *Compas* at the Holy Sepulchre Church, the tomb of Christ in Jerusalem. Others assert that due east is the proper direction because Christ will emerge from that quarter of the heavens in glory at the Second Coming. In 1823, William Wordsworth alluded to this in an orientational poem quoted below.

Early Christian buildings followed Jewish and Pagan tradition in having a westward alignment – an occidentation. Before the destruction of the temple in Jerusalem in the year 70, and the dispersal of the Jews in the Diaspora, Jews directed their prayers towards the west, the liturgical direction of the *shekhinah*, God's presence. Following Jewish tradition, the original church of the Holy Sepulchre in Jerusalem, built in the fourth century by the Emperor Constantine at the Christian *omphalos* of the world, the *Compas*, faced west. So do the two holiest churches in Rome – San Giovanni in

Laterano (St John Lateran, consecrated in the year 324) and San Pietro in Vaticano (St Peter's in the Vatican, 326). The third great anciently founded church of imperial Rome, Santa Maria Maggiore (358), has its orientation to the north-west, not easterly. But this very early occidentation did not last, leaving these churches and the successors built on their sites as rarities. Orientation, alignment towards the east, goes back to at least the fifth century, for the *Apostolic Constitutions* of the year 472 ordered churches to be built to a rectangular plan with the head to the east.

Continental medieval writers such as Giulielmus (William) Durandus in his *Symbolism of Churches* state that churches should face due east. Durandus himself complained that some faced solstitial sunrise, which is far off equinoctial east-west. Many medieval churches, especially in northern Europe, are orientated roughly eastwards, but certainly not on the equinoctial line. Rare examples where one is equinoctial are notable for that reason. Seemingly, the reason for the variation in church orientations is recorded nowhere in the canonical writings of the church.

It has long been asserted by antiquaries that at least some churches are orientated towards sunrise on their patronal festivals, the calendar day of the saint to which the church is dedicated. There are thousands of medieval churches in Europe whose original dedications are known. Some are certainly equinoctial, though this may be an orientation for the day of the Annunication of the Blessed Virgin Mary, at the spring equinox in medieval times. Two significant churches dedicated to Our Lady have this orientation. Salisbury Cathedral, the Cathedral Church of St Mary, whose foundation stone was laid on the 28th of April 1220, is oriented 'between the equinoxes', due east-west. As can be seen from the sundial on the south side, the Frauenkirche in Munich, founded in 1488, is very close to a true east-west orientation.

If a church is founded facing the rising sun on its saint's day, then the sun will rise directly in front of it on every subsequent saint's day. In the long run, though, as the calendar drifts away from the sun as the result of accumulated inaccuracies and the precession of the equinoxes, the orientation will be lost. But this is a very long process.

Another suggestion for the underlying principle of orientation is magnetic. The earliest known reference to a magnet is from the Roman poet Lucretius (c.58 BCE), who tells how the lodestone draws iron towards it. It was long known by blacksmiths that an iron bar, hammered in a north-south orientation, would take on the Earth's *megin* and become *magnat* – magnetized. The earliest reference to the magnetic compass, however, is by the Englishman Alexander Neckham in 1187, when it was already being used in navigation. So it is quite possible that the magnetic compass could have been used in medieval church orientation. There are a number of medieval churches in England whose orientations might have been determined with the magnetic compass. Chichester Cathedral's orientation is related to magnetic north-south at the time of its foundation, in 1108.

By the 1400s, European compasses were marked out with a blue cross for the cardinal points, and a red cross for the intercardinals. The East was marked by a cross, which may indicate the use of the compass for finding the direction of Christian prayer, or perhaps for architectural orientation. North became the primary direction for maps and compasses later.

Whether or not it was used in medieval times for orientation, in later years, the magnetic compass was used geomantically in Europe. As the first full description in Europe of a Chinese geomantic compass was published in the *Museum Wormianum*, in Leyden, the Netherlands in March 1655, this usage may reflect an interest in Chinoiserie. In 1735, the period when interest in Feng-Shui (as *Sharawadgi*) led Sir William Chambers to erect a pagoda in Kew Gardens, the grave of the English antiquary Thomas Hearne was orientated by compass. Later, in 1811, the main axis of Regent's Park in London was aligned on magnetic north-south by John Nash. None of these instances prove a pre-1655 use of the compass in European orientation.

At the Reformation, certain Puritans strove to abolish every Christian custom that had no biblical precedent. This process took place over more than a century, culminating in the banning of Christmas by Oliver Cromwell's regime. In practice, there were few deliberate misorientations of churches after the formation of the Church of England, but in Cambridge, the chapel of Emmanuel College was an instance of this. In 1584, the fanatical Protestant Sir Walter Mildmay set up a new college in the buildings of a former Dominican Priory that had been suppressed in 1538. To defy Catholic practice, he made the old medieval chapel, which was orientated properly, into a dining

King's College Chapel south side, west end

hall. The old dining hall, orientated north-south, he converted into the college chapel. This new chapel was criticised at the time for its misorientation, and it was never actually consecrated. In the 1660s, after the restoration of the old order, a new chapel was built, designed by Sir Christopher Wren, and orientated properly.

Because much of the craftsman's knowledge of church orientation had been destroyed by the Reformation and later Cromwellian Puritanism, seventeenth century English antiquaries attempted to piece together the broken tradition once more. One of them was Silas Taylor, a.k.a. Domville. As a captain in Cromwell's Parliamentary army, Taylor/Domville built up a fine collection of ancient manuscripts. During the Civil War, his detachment looted the cathedral libraries at Hereford and Worcester, and his knowledge of orientation probably came from some of these illicitly acquired ancient ecclesiastical writings. One manuscript, sold at his death in 1678, had the passage, 'In the days of yore, when a church was to be built, they watched and prayed on the vigil of the dedication, and took that point of the horizon where the sun arose from the East, which makes that variation so that few stand true, except those built between the two equinoxes. I have experimented some churches, and have found the line to point to that part of the horizon where the sun arises on the day of that Saint to whom the church is dedicated.'

A Scottish Masonic tradition, recorded by W.A. Laurie in *The History of Free Masonry and the Grand Lodge of Scotland*, (1859) tells us: 'On the evening previous, the Patrons, Ecclesiastics and Masons assembled and spent the night in devotional exercises: one being placed to watch the rising of the sun, gave notice when his rays appeared above the horizon. When fully in view, the Master Mason sent out a man with a rod, which he ranged in line between the altar and the sun, and thus fixed a line of orientation.'

The English poet William Wordsworth (1770–1850) was involved in choosing the location for the church of St Mary at Rydal in the English Lake District. The chapel has a remarkable location, chosen with exquisite sensibility for the form of the landscape and traditional English church geomancy. 'How fondly with the woods embrace this daughter of thy pious care', wrote the poet.

In 1823, Wordsworth wrote two poems dedicated to Lady Le Fleming, the chapel's founder, who laid the foundation stone in July that year. It was consecrated by the Bishop of Chester, Dr Blomfield, on August 25, 1825. Wordsworth's poems are titled *On Seeing the Foundation Preparing for the Erection of Rydal Chapel, Westmorland*, and *On the Same Occasion.* They were published in 1827. In a note to the second poem, Wordsworth wrote: 'Our churches, invariably, perhaps, stand east and west, but why is by few persons *exactly* known; nor, that the degree of deviation from due east often noticeable in the ancient ones was determined, in each particular case, by the point in the horizon, at which the sun rose upon the day of the saint to whom the church was dedicated.' He tells of this in the poem:

When in the antique age of bow and spear
And feudal rapine clothed with iron mail,
Came ministers of peace, intent to rear
The Mother Church in yon sequestered vale;

Then, to her Patron Saint, a previous rite
Resounded with deep swell and solemn close,
Through unremitting vigils of the night,
Till from his couch the wished-for Sun uprose.

He rose, and straight – as by divine command,
They, who had waited for the sign to trace
Their work's foundation, gave with careful hand
To the high altar its determined place.

Mindful of Him Who in the Orient born
There lived, and on the cross His life resigned,
And Who, from out the regions of the morn,
Issuing in pomp, shall come to judge mankind.

Research into the orientation of churches remains fraught with difficulties. The date of foundation must be known accurately, and then the position of sunrise calculated in the old Julian calendar, taking into account the height of the horizon relative to the church. Sometimes, as at King's, the foundation-stone was not laid on the saint's day. Then again, church dedications have often been altered over the years, and local factors of landscape and townscape may play their part. In the 1950s, the Reverend Hugh Benson attempted to gain useful statistics by studying British church orientations systematically. A good proportion of churches he studied did conform to the patronal day sunrise orientations, but by no means all of them. So the outcome of his work was inconclusive.

The problems of the meaning of orientation are explicit at Cambridge, where the details of the foundation and dedication of King's College Chapel are a matter of record. In 1853, J. Rigg of the Cambridge Antiquarian Society determined that King's College Chapel, founded by King Henry VI on the 25th of July, 1446, has an orientation that corresponds with sunrise on the 22nd of March in that year. Its patronal days are the 25th of March and the 6th of December, dedicated to Our Lady and St Nicholas, respectively. The foundation-stone, however, was laid by the king on neither holy day, but on the 25th of July, St James's Day. This causes problems as to whether the orientation was determined on the day of foundation, or that of laying the foundation-stone. A similar problem exists with Salisbury Cathedral.

If we do not just reject the 'saint's day' theory as inappropriate in this case, then there are a number of possible explanations for this orientation. The chapel of King's College was founded in the middle of an existing town, the king having demolished an old church, St John's Zachary, and houses to clear the site. If the founders viewed the rising sun over the roofs of the houses to the east as a direct observational necessity, then the orientational difference may be accounted for. Another, less likely, possibility is that the foundations were prepared on the 22nd of March, and the orientation fixed from scaffolding erected so that the locators could view the sun over the rooftops. The new chapel may have followed the general orientation of the old St John's church. Or, perhaps the whole idea of spot-on accuracy of alignment is a projection back into a past when it was not considered important.

When we compare Christian church orientation with the traditional Moslem rule-of-thumb methods to determine the direction of Mecca, which also originates in medieval tradition, the rules-of-thumb for finding the *qiblah* are certainly less accurate than a three-day difference of angle in a medieval Christian chapel. But they are not considered a hindrance to ritual correctness in Islam, and perhaps the same leeway was permitted in Christian orientation. Because Islam stresses the importance of prayer towards Mecca, its tradition has been maintained, whilst Christian orientation has never, so far as can be told, had the same ritual geomantic significance. The psychological need for accuracy of a greater order for things other than weights and measures may have originated in the Renaissance, whose world-view had not arrived in England in 1446. Recorded instances of electional astrology in England are post-medieval, though it is quite possible that important buildings like King's College Chapel could have had the times of their foundations elected by astrologers. But there is no documentary evidence of this.

In *Appendix E* of his *King's College Chapel: Notes on its History and Present Condition* (1867), 'On the orientation of King's College Chapel', Thomas John Proctor Carter writes:

It is generally considered that the mediaeval builders made their churches point to that part of the horizon where the sun rose on the day of the foundation of the church, which was also that of the patron saint. Mr Rigg discusses the application of this theory to King's College Chapel in one of the *Cambridge Antiquarian Communications* (Vol. I. p. 59). He writes: 'The direction of the ridge of King's College Chapel (according to Professor Adams) is 60 degrees 20 minutes 3 seconds to the North of East. The sun rises at this point of the compass when his declination is 30 degrees 53 minutes North. This takes place at present on 31st March and 13th September. Now, at the date of the foundation of the chapel, this difference between the Old and New Styles would be nine days. Therefore the corresponding dates are 22nd March and 4th September.' Mr Rigg proceeds to argue that the theory of orientation is irreconcilable with this.

As we have seen, the foundation stone was laid on the 25th of July. It was, however, probably laid after the lines of the building had been drawn out and the foundations begun, while the day must have been chosen to suit the

King's College Chapel, cherubim and tetragrammaton

> king's convenience. We cannot therefore decide what the actual day of the foundation was. The principal patron is Saint Mary, and we should therefore expect that the day chosen to direct the orientation would be the 25th of March. An error of three days may very probably be due to inaccuracy of observation. Mr Rigg, however, considers that the builders adopted the direction of due East, and calculated from the vernal equinox on the 21st of March, which of course involves a much smaller error. Such may have been the method in this instance, although unquestionably it was not a general practice. But whether or no the above-stated theory is correct, the case of this chapel cannot be safely alleged against it.

The matter of the chapel's orientation is complicated by the fact that it was partially constructed over the site of an earlier church. The orientation of the former church of St. John's Zachary, over the sanctuary of which the west end of the chapel was built, has not been determined. It is possible that the chapel continued the orientation by using part of the foundations of the old church. But whether this was done is not known. Medieval extensions of existing churches often had orientations that differed from the original building, the so-called 'deflected chancel'. This is where an eastward extension of the church, built later than the nave, is on a different orientation. Sometimes, the orientation differs by a remarkable amount, so there must have been a good reason for the change. An example of a deflected chancel can be seen at Great St. Mary's, almost opposite King's. Another church in the Cambridge region with this feature is St Nicholas at Trumpington.

Until the sacrosanct King's Lawn is excavated, the possibility remains that the orientation of King's Chapel was a continuation of that of St. John's Zachary. In any case, King's College Chapel represents a definite eastward extension of the original axis of St. John's Zachary, carrying on the alignment laid out centuries before. That God's House had been set up on this part of the site is evidence that it had previous sanctity. But once the chapel was built, the locus was transformed into a sacred place of a higher order.

Freemasonry

In *A Short Account of* King's College Chapel (1921), under the heading, *Work of Freemasons*, W.P. Littlechild wrote: 'It may be that some of my readers are members of the Masonic body.' Mr. John Proctor Carter, sometime fellow of King's and Eton, in writing a history of the chapel, published in 1867, writes thus:

> So many learned authors have been at fault when they have ventured into the obscurity which envelops the history of the Freemasons, by a gang of whom this chapel, in common with, at all events, a large number of mediaeval buildings were erected, that to say a word upon the subject may seem presumptuous. The theory of a traditional science, confined entirely to the members of a secret society that had ramified over the whole of civilised Europe, and to whom developments in architecture were due, has been pushed to extremity by some writers. By a natural reaction others have been led to discredit altogether the existence of such a society, and to consider the Masonic fraternity merely as one of the various trade corporations or guilds whose relics have descended to our own day. But apart from the argument drawn from universal belief, there is probably sufficient evidence to show that the Freemasons were distinguished to some extent from other guilds, partly by the possession of peculiar secrets, and partly by their religious character. They seem to have been as it were the knight-errants of architecture, and to have travelled from city to city and country to country in the exercise of what

> they must have deemed a half sacred profession. Ample proof has been adduced that Henry VI was not only a Mason himself (having been admitted a member of the fraternity in 1450), but did a good deal for the craft; and Freemasonry has much to thank him for.

Masons' marks are to be found in various places on the walls in the chapel. Representative examples are reproduced here.

King's College Chapel, operative masons' marks

Chapter 9

Name and Number

Sacred Numerology, Gematria and Geometry

Folklore and commentators alike frequently stress the importance of symbolic number in churches. There are numerous instances of churches whose numbers of windows, pillars, niches, pinnacles and bays reproduce the number of months, weeks and days of the year. For example, St Paul's Cathedral in London is equal in height, in feet, to the number of days in the year. In her highly speculative Druidical book *Prehistoric London: Its Mounds and Circles*, (1925) Elizabeth Gordon writes of Henry VI: 'It is recorded that the King frequently attended Divine Service in St Mary's College Chapel and impressed with the beautiful proportions, the sacred numbers employed in the "days" of the large windows and the ground plan in the form of the ancient T-shaped cross, determined to reproduce Wykeham's plans in every detail, only on a more magnificent scale, for his own colleges at Eton and Cambridge.' St Mary's College Chapel is part of Winchester College, or the School of St Mary Winton, founded by William of Wykeham in the time of King Edward III according to spiritual principles.

Once the site for King's College Chapel was cleared, the job of laying out the ground-plan was carried out by Reginald Ely and his assistants. The centre-line of the building was laid out on the determined orientation, however that was determined. The two hundred and eighty-eight foot length of the plan seems to have been laid out by twelve circles of twelve foot radius centred upon this line (twelve times twelve times two being the full internal length). From analysis of the chapel's dimensions, it appears that a module of four English feet was used. Thus, the radius of each circle was made out by three modules, making each severy (bay) measure six modules (twenty-four feet) by ten modules (forty feet), giving a total ground area of seven hundred and twenty square modules. In modular terms, the ground plan is divided into twelve integral Pythagorean triangles with sides of five, twelve and thirteen units.

The number twelve is recurrent in the numerical scheme. There are twelve severies (bays) in the layout of the chapel, each twelve by two feet in length, with four octagonal corner towers and twenty-two buttresses, twenty-six uprights in all. There are twelve great claves (ceiling bosses), one in the centre of each severy. Above each great side window are three quatrefoil lights in square settings. These allow light into the corridor which runs in the wall above the windows. There are seventy-two in all (twelve times six). From these two corridors, twenty-four entrances (one per severy, two times twelve) allow access to the top of the vaulting, whose thickness at the thinnest part is a only a few inches (half an inch or six inches, according to differing accounts).

The number of fleurons above the small windows and at the ends are seventy-two for the lights plus twelve (eighty-four equals twelve times seven). Lozenges above the side chantries are two hundred and sixteen (twelve times eighteen). Fleurons per tower are eight, making thirty-two in all, whilst fleurons above the side chantries are one hundred and eight (twelve times nine). In each end window, there are eighteen major panels (called 'days' in the original contract), thirty-six in all (twelve times three). Of the intermediate pierced pinnacles on the side walls, there are thirty-six per side, seventy-two (twelve times six) in all. The dimensions of the side windows are formed from square numbers. They are sixteen feet (the square of four) in width, and forty-nine feet (the square of seven) high.

King Henry's will stipulated that the side chapels, each 'a closet with an altar therein' as he put it, should measure 'in length 20 feet and in breadth 10 feet vaulted and finished'. However, each side-chapel actually measures twenty feet six inches by twelve feet, a dimension produced according to the geometrical system of *ad triangulum* by inscribing a hexagram in a circle. Apart from the small variations in measurement occurring through various inaccuracies in construction, this seems to be the major departure from the stipulated dimensions of the founder. Just as with the case of orientation, such inaccuracies make it difficult to be categorical about the precise intended geometry of very large sacred buildings such as this. As with the Islamic rule-of-thumb for finding the *qiblah*, it is likely that intention, rather than modern ideas of instrumental accuracy, was the goal. Even contemporary buildings, in an age of complex and precise instrumentation, based upon accurate plans, show such variations.

Medieval builders sometimes used a device which may have been used since antiquity, which had the advantage of being easy to use, but the disadvantage of dimensional inaccuracy. This is the so-called Druid's Cord, a rope with twelve knots and thirteen sections. This basic tool enables us to lay out a right-angled triangle with sections three, four and five units long without measurement. An alternative, sometimes used in Masonic ceremonies, is to use three rods, one measuring three feet, one four and one five. When brought together by three men, a right-angle is formed. Of course, one of the ancient emblems of masonry is the square, a right-angled tool, and the other emblem, a pair of compasses. These are used in the squaring and subsequent working of the stones of the building. By practical measurement, medieval craftsmen were able to lay out a tolerably accurate ground-plan, on which was built a physical manifestation of number and proportion in brick, stone and timber.

Henry Malden, in his 1769 guidebook, wrote enigmatically of the masons who built the chapel:

> They have left, I am told, in the course of their work, certain marks very well known to all adepts of their

> society. What these monuments of Masonry may be, I am unable to declare; but refer my reader, if he is learned in the secrets of that fraternity, to an inspection of every mysterious token about the building. One thing, however, I shall mention, which has often been observed – that in the South Porch of the chapel there are *three* steps, at the west door, *five* and in the north porch *seven*. These are numbers, with the mystery or at least with the sound of which Free-Masons are said to be particularly well-acquainted.

The ground plan is composed of three pairs of Pythagorean triangles, each twenty-four by ten by twenty-six modules. This figure twenty-six (two times thirteen), is one of the guiding numerical principles of the building. On the west end, this is expressed in the early seventeenth century carving of the tetragrammaton – the Hebrew characters JHVH, the secret name of God. In Kabbalistic gematria, the letters J, H, V, H represent the numbers ten, five, six and five, which add up to twenty-six.

The chapel itself has twenty-six great windows of painted glass and twenty-six structural uprights, but not one free-standing pillar. Of window tracery in the eighteen small side-chapels, each side has thirteen rounded portions, and five rectilinear, giving twenty-six and ten respectively. Inside the chapel, each pair of fans in the vaulting has twenty-six ribs. In the ante-chapel, the tracery of each interior side-chapel window has twelve rounded and fourteen long parts, twenty-six in all. On each of the two doors in the choir, there are twelve crockets (six per side), and one pinnacle, twenty-six in all.

Both the Hebrew and the Greek alphabets are instances of an ancient means of notation where alphabetic characters stand for numbers. This is not an easy thing to grasp, because the Romans, whose alphabet we use, developed a separate system of numbers that are strictly utilitarian. Similarly, the Arabic numerals we use today have no alphabetic equivalent.

The ancient Greek philosopher Pythagoras and his followers saw number as the guiding principle of the Cosmos. Through number, the emanations of physical existence came into being. Number was thus essential to the process or realization. The Pythagoreans and the Hebrews both used the decimal system of notation, but without the key concept of zero.

The Hebrew and Greek alphabets are both significant in the Christian religion, because these are the languages that the scriptures were written in. To Jewish mystics, the scriptures are the revelation of God. They can be read on a number of levels; literal, symbolic, philosophical and numerical. Each word, each name in Hebrew and Greek, also represents a number. This is seen as the true cosmic nature of the thing so represented, an aspect of the divine gnosis contained in words and numbers. The art of using this system is called gematria. When reading a word or seeing an image and knowing its Greek (or Hebrew) name, one can add up the number-equivalents of the alphabetic characters in the name to produce a sum. This number can then be found to represent other Greek (or Hebrew) words or names which then are viewed as divinely connected.

The *New Testament* was written originally in Greek, and hence the names and qualities in it have a numerical interpretation. St Irenaeus noted that the number-equivalents of the Greek word for 'dove' and Alpha and Omega are eight hundred and one. Thus, the dove can be taken, through numerical equivalents of its name, as signifying 'the first and the last', or, in its esoteric interpretation, negotiable (earthly) wealth and immutable (heavenly) wealth. In turn, eight hundred and one is three times two hundred and sixty seven, which is the number of the Greek word for the Kingdom. The Kingdom's number multiplied by ten is equivalent to the Greek for 'The Lord of Light', 'The Light of the World', 'The Church of Jesus Christ' and 'The Great Power of Light' – two thousand, six hundred and seventy.

These numerical connections, well documented in Jewish and Byzantine writings, provide an occult mystical link between the key concepts of religion. All other Pagan, Jewish and Christian symbols may be interpreted in this way, through the number of their name. The notorious 'Number of the Beast' from the

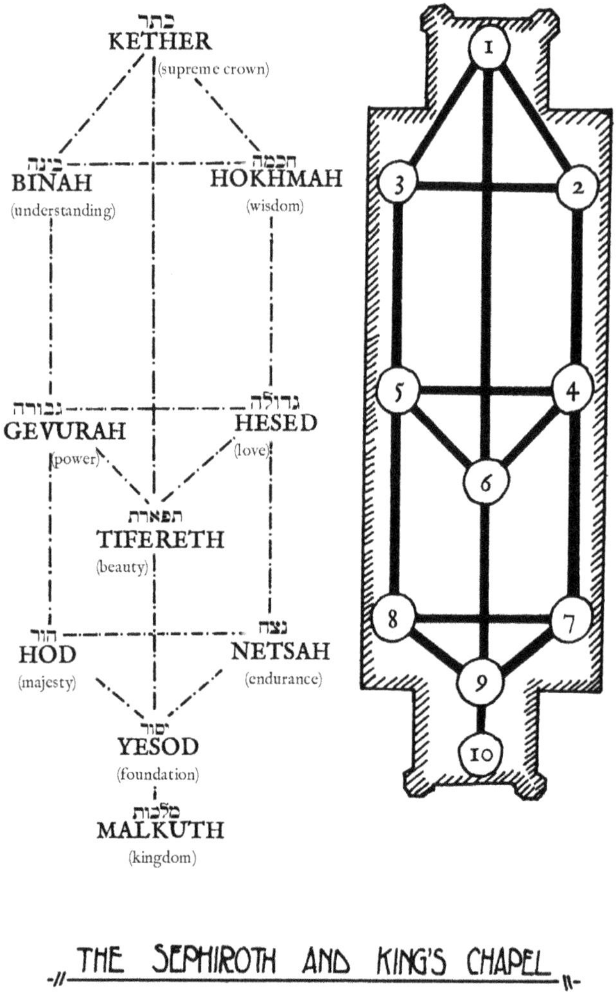
כתר
KETHER
(supreme crown)
בינה
BINAH
(understanding)
חכמה
HOKHMAH
(wisdom)
גבורה
GEVURAH
(power)
גדולה
HESED
(love)
תפארת
TIFERETH
(beauty)
הוד
HOD
(majesty)
נצח
NETSAH
(endurance)
יסוד
YESOD
(foundation)
מלכות
MALKUTH
(kingdom)
1
2
3
4
5
6
7
8
9
10
THE SEPHIROTH AND KING'S CHAPEL

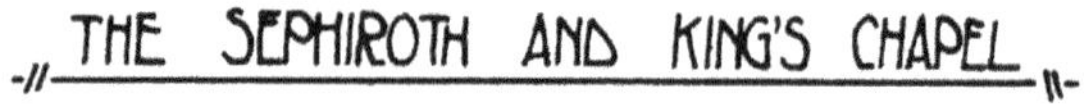

King's College Chapel, Sephiroth analogy diagram

Revelation of St John is the best-known instance of gematria, though its meaning has been much disputed over the centuries.

This link between numerology and dedication is also expressed in the length of the chapel, as ordered by its founder. It can be interpreted in terms of the Jewish Kabbalah, though there is no overt reference to this in the ancient texts about the chapel. In feet, the length two hundred and eighty-eight is equal to the numbers of the two kabbalistic sephiroth Hesed and Gevurah. Hesed's number is seventy-two, and Gevurah's is two hundred and sixteen. Respectively they signify mercy and power. Hesed is masculine and Gevurah feminine, just as the complete dedication is to St. Nicholas (mercy) and Our Lady (power). The combination of Hesed and Gevurah gives forth 'beauty' – the harmonious balance expressed in the Chapel's proportions.

The numbers of names generated in Greek gematria appear in the ratios present in sacred geometry. The ruling geometrical schema of the ground-plan of King's College Chapel is *ad triangulum*, based upon the equilateral triangle and its developed forms. The vesica, a geometric figure produced by the intersection of two equal-diameter circles through their centres, as the fish is an esoteric symbol of the Christian religion. The Greek words for Saviour and fish, Soter and ichthus, have the relationship 1408:1219, which is an excellent approximation to the ratio of the diameter of a circle to the side of an equilateral triangle inscribed within the circle. This ratio is actually two to the square root of three. The cross produced within this diagram has arms measuring six hundred and nine point six units, whose nearest integral number, six hundred and ten, is equivalent in gematria to a word meaning 'the cross'. Gematria gives a meaningful mystery to geometric proportions. At its most developed, gematrial proportions in sacred buildings can infuse every part with symbolic meaning. Unseen and unrecognized by the casual visitor, or even the devout worshipper,

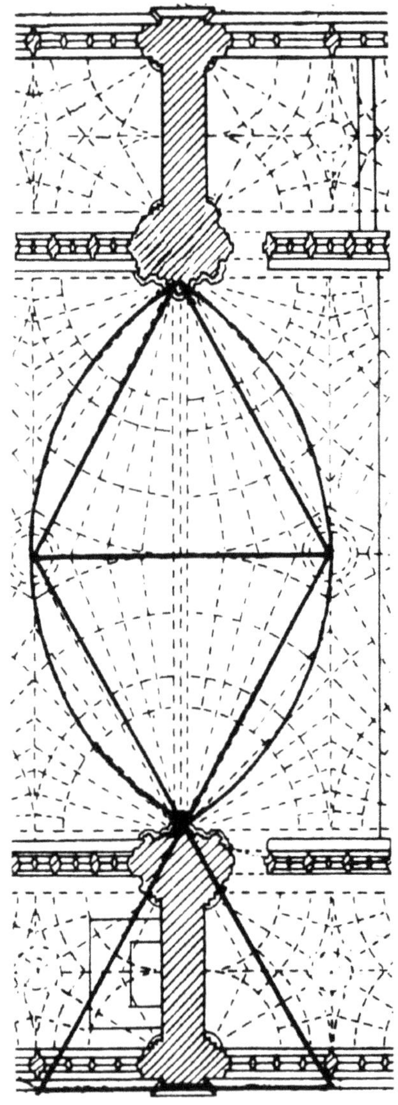

King's College Chapel sacred geometry, equilateral triangles and vesica piscis defining transverse proportions and main vault

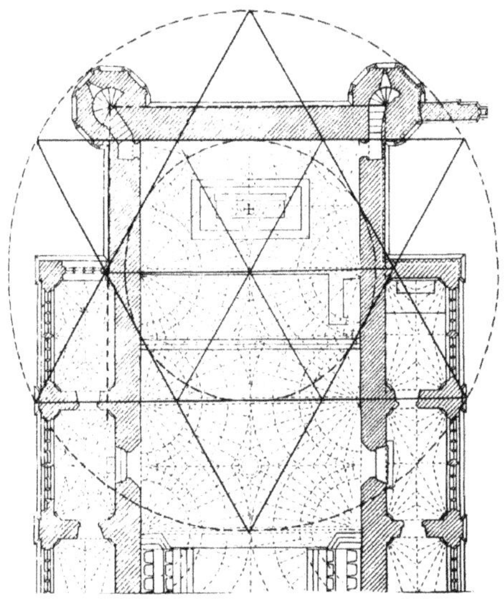

King's College Chapel, sacred geometry, east end

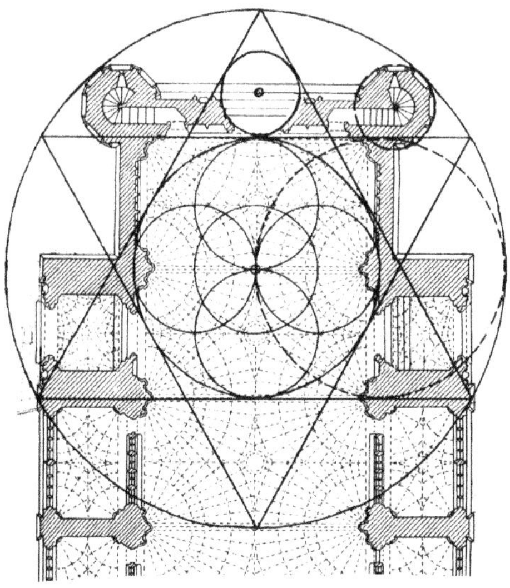

King's College Chapel, sacred geometry, west end

these proportions are an allegory of the unseen divine working in every part of the cosmos, from the largest to the smallest level.

In Christian symbolism, the ante-chapel as far as the steps can be seen to represent the Old Covenant of the Jewish Old Testament. When one goes up the steps and through the screen into the choir, one has entered the New Covenant of

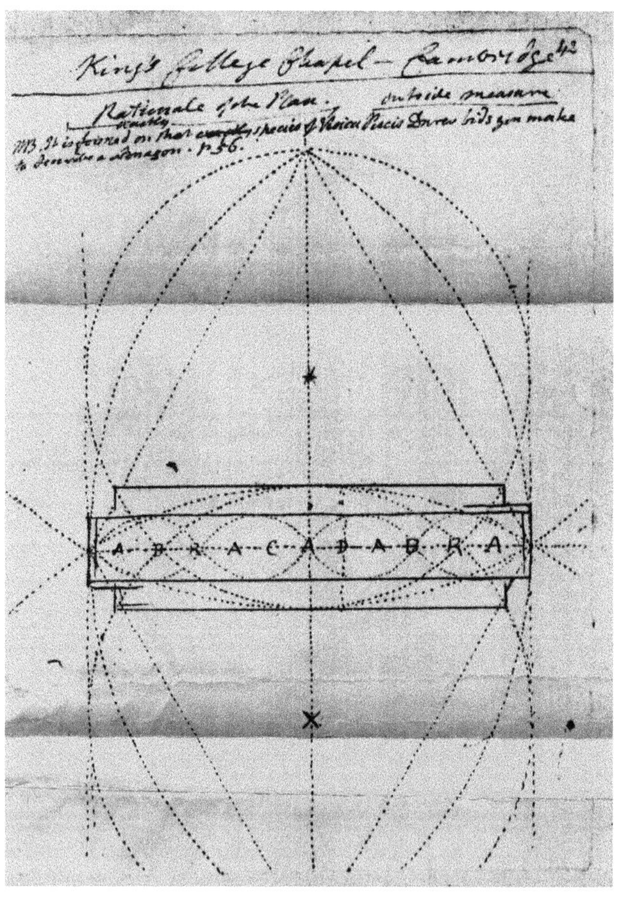

A nineteenth century manuscript with an esoteric analysis of the sacred geometry of King's College Chapel

Christianity and the New Testament. The tabernacles flanking the west door have pillars to support images. These images were never made, owing to the advent of Protestantism. These tabernacles are emblematic of the pillars named Boaz and Jachin, which stood before the entrance of the Temple in Jerusalem. The Jewish connection is emphasised by the early seventeenth century carving of the tetragrammaton over the west door.

William Wordsworth, who had a finely developed sense of the spiritual in architecture, wrote three of his Ecclesiastical Sketches (better known after 1837 as *Ecclesiastical Sonnets*) about King's College Chapel. The first two deal with the chapel, while the third speaks also of Westminster Abbey and St Paul's Cathedral. Possibly, all three were composed in Cambridge in November or December 1820. They were published in 1822.

Ecclesiastical Sonnet XLIII: Inside of King's College Chapel, Cambridge

Tax not the Royal Saint with vain expense,
With ill-matched aims the Architect who planned –
Albeit labouring for a scanty band
Of white-robed Scholars only – this immense
And glorious Work of fine intelligence!
Give all thou canst; high Heaven rejects the lore

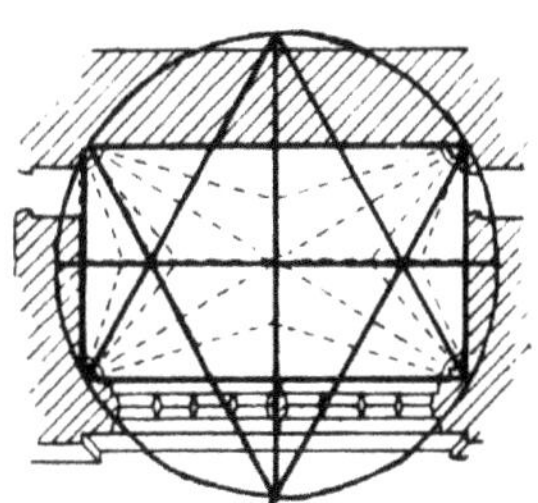
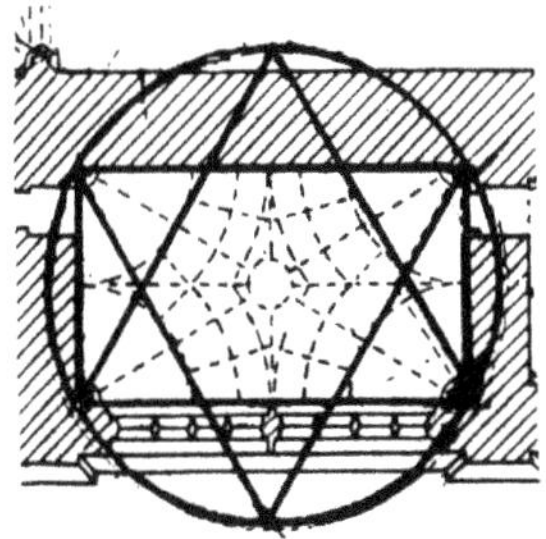

Geometric definition of the side chapels

Of nicely-calculated less or more;
So deemed the man who fashioned for the sense
These lofty pillars, spread that branching roof
Self-poised, and scooped into ten thousand cells,
Where light and shade repose, where music dwells
Lingering – and wandering on as loth to die;
Like thoughts whose very sweetness yieldeth proof
That they were born for immortality.

XLIV The Same

What awful perspective! while from our sight
With gradual stealth the lateral windows hide
Their Portraitures, their stone-work glimmers, dyed
In the soft chequerings of a sleepy light.
Martyr, or King, or sainted Eremite,
Whoe'er ye be, that thus, yourselves unseen,
Imbue your prison-bars with solemn sheen,
Shine on, until ye fade, with coming Night.
But from the arms of silence – list! O list!
The music bursteth into second life;
The notes luxuriate, every stone is kissed
By sound, or ghost of sound, in mazy strife;
Heart-thrilling strains, that cast, before the eye
Of the devout, a veil of ecstasy!

XLV Continued

They dreamt not of a perishable home
Who thus could build. Be mine, in hours of fear,
Or grovelling thought, to seek a refuge here;
Or through the aisles of Westminster to roam;
Where bubbles burst, and folly's dancing foam
Melts, if it cross the threshold; where the wreath
Of awe-struck wisdom droops: or let my path
Lead to that younger Pile, whose sky-like dome
Hath typified by reach of daring art

Infinity's embrace; whose guardian crest,
The silent Cross, among the stars shall spread
As now, She hath also seen her breast
Filled with mementoes, satiate with its part
Of grateful England's overflowing dead.

As the Catholic religious aspect of life faded due to the Reformation, the chapel was reaching completion. It was never finished, as it belonged to quite a different world-view than the post-Reformation one. The ritual had changed, obviating the need for seventeen altars, which were destroyed. The chantries had been suppressed, so no more prayers were offered for the souls of the departed in Purgatory. The colour intended was absent, and, as the years passed, the vestments were abolished, the language was changed from Latin to English, the incense was stopped, the music altered, then removed. Relics were grubbed out of the resting-places, and even the foundation-stone was lost.

As the integrated culture of the Catholic religion was destroyed, and the economic power of the monasteries obliterated, so, with the emergence of capitalism, financiers and bankers became increasingly important in British society. No longer were Christians forbidden to lend money, the sin of usury was no longer considered relevant, and economic considerations of space caused expedient designs to be adopted for new sacred buildings. For a while, even the orientation of churches was deliberately defied, as at the Puritan Emmanuel College.

In Britain, the understanding of the meaning and nature of medieval sacred architecture was gradually downgraded after the Reformation. New styles of building, based on antique Roman principles, were introduced. Their system of proportion, delineated by Vitruvius, made canonical by Alberti and Palladio, and widely circulated in sumptuously-illustrated books, was considered superior to the systems of the medieval builders, which were continued now only by the guilds of carpenters making timber buildings. So by 1624, in his *Elements of Architecture*, Henry Wotton could call the medieval

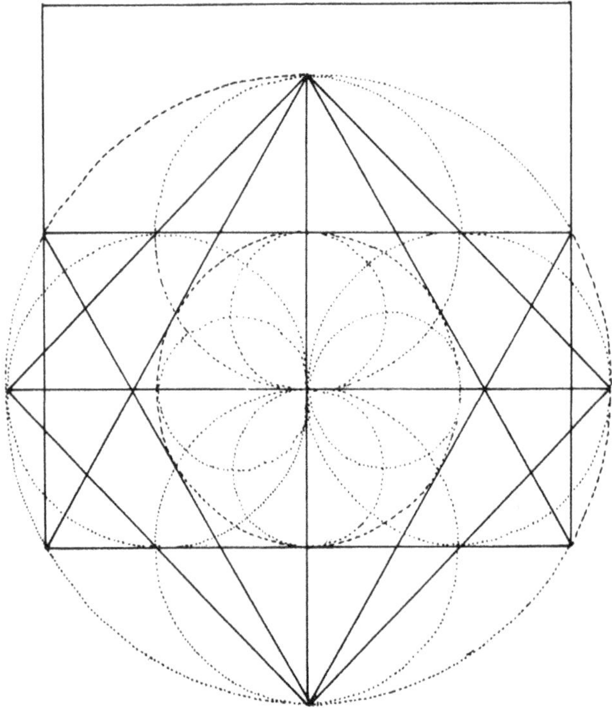

The 24 foot radius inner circle drawn at the junction of two severies is the basis of the interpenetrating equilateral triangles upon which the total width of the chapel is based (84 feet). The equilateral triangle delineates the junction of the third and fourth severy, and a further equilateral triangle projected from the first marks with its base the mid-point of the chapel. The whole length of the chapel is based upon six 24 foot radius circles. The circle circumscribed round the two equilateral triangles (96 feet diameter) delineates the edges of the end towers. Thus the ground plan of King's College Chapel is 'ad triangulum', the Flemish and German system of church construction. The side chapels are each based on a 12 foot radius outer circle with sides based upon inscribed interpenetrating equilateral triangles.

King's College Chapel, sacred geometry

architecture he loathed by the insulting name of 'Gothic'. 'This form, both for the natural imbecility of the sharp angle itself, and likewise for its very uncomelinesse, ought to be exiled from judicious eyes, and left to its first inventors, the Gothes and Lombardes, among other reliques of that barbarous age.' Not wishing to perpetuate Wotton's prejudice, or indeed his false history, I do not use the prejudiced name 'Gothic' to describe medieval Christian architecture.

After Wotton, King's College Chapel became a spectacle, despite its sacred canonical dimensions, and no longer recognized as a unique instrument for enlightenment. The principle of the temple, as the microcosm of the macrocosmic Creation, was lost sight of, and spiritual science was rejected by the majority of churchmen, becoming restricted to the secretive circles of speculative freemasons and scholars of Hermetic and Rosicrucian leanings. Buildings were demolished in front of the chapel, and vistas were opened up in the new spirit of the 'picturesque'. Lack of funds prevented the realization of the rest of the scheme. The consecrated cemetery, which had been the churchyard of St. John's Zachary, had become part of 'The Backs', a bowling green, and is now part of what is known as King's Lawn.

Since the eighteenth century, the public attitude towards the chapel is in terms of 'art'. The nineteenth century art commentator and theorist John Ruskin was a very severe critic of the chapel, comparing it to 'a billiard table turned upside down', when there were no billiard tables in the fifteenth century. If Ruskin had played billiards or snooker, he would have known that the proportions of a billiard table are quite different than those of the chapel. Ruskin's generally perceptive understanding of architecture seems to have broken down completely in Cambridge. However, John Proctor Carter asserted: 'It is entitled to be ranked with the finest buildings of the world.' The present author agrees with Carter.

When the original edition of this book appeared in 1974, I noted that 'angular concrete is all that is permitted as architectural'. Fortunately, times have changed, and the third-hand imitation of middle-period Le Corbusier copyists, the belated followers of the 'New Brutalists', sub-Bauhaus rhetoriticians and notorious failures like the History Faculty Building can now be seen as just the fashionable styles of the third quarter of the twentieth century in Cambridge. Despite forays

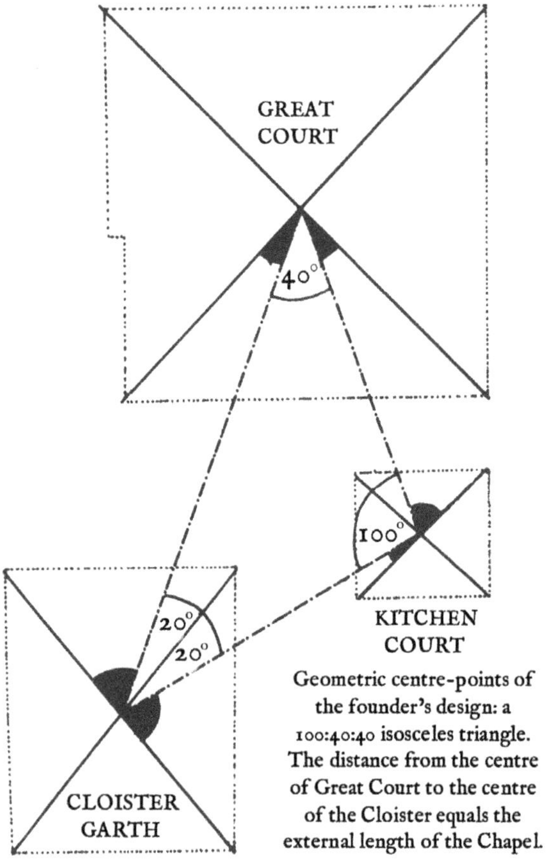

King's College founder's plan, ground geometry

into postmodern ironic quotation, 'The Architecture of the Jumping Universe' , 'hi-tech', 'freestyle' and 'ecstatic architecture', there is now a growing recognition that the ancient is not entirely worthless in its own right, and is more than just 'heritage' to be preserved for the tourists. Hopefully, we have learned sufficiently from the results of postmodern excess not to imitate Las Vegas.

A Arabic

H Hebrew

G Greek

L Latin

ON Old Norse

BRACE Timber component completing a triangle to create a rigid structure

CALM (OR CAME) The channelled lead strip that supports plain, coloured, painted and stained glass in a window

CARDO The north-south road of a Roman town (L)

COLLAR-BEAM Horizontal timber connecting a pair of rafters at a point below the apex

COMPAS The Christian centre of the world

DAMP COURSE A continuous course of impervious material in a wall just above ground level, preventing damp from the ground from rising up through the structure

DANELAW The part of England under Danish rule after the year 878

GEMATRIA The art of numerology, deriving numbers from names and words in Hebrew and Greek

GUILD A legally-protected association of craftsmen

HARAM A Muslim holy place, protected by the law of sanctuary (A)

HYTHE A riverside quay used for loading and unloading ships

MAGNAT Anything that has become empowered with megin (q.v.), hence 'magnet', a stone empowered with megin (ON)

MEGIN Indwelling empowerment that emanates from the spiritual nature of a being or body (ON)

OMPHALOS The 'navel' or centre of the world (G)

ORIENTATION The direction of something towards the east

QIBLAH The orientation of Moslem prayer towards Mecca (A)

REREDOS Ornamental screen at the back of an altar

SHEKHINAH The presence of God (H)

VEBOND A ceremonial fence of hazel staves surrounding the sacred enclosure of a heathen holy place (ON)

Anon, *154 Views of Cambridge*, Valentine & Sons, Birmingham, n.d. (c. 1900)

Aquinas, Thomas (trans. Thomas Gilby), *Philosophical Texts*, Oxford University Press, New York, 1960

Bucher, Francois, *Architector: The Lodge Books and Sketchbooks of Medieval Architects*, Abaris Books, New York, 1979

Bligh Bond, Frederick, & Lea, Thomas Simcox, *Gematria: A Preliminary Investigation of the Cabala contained in the Coptic Gnostic Books*, Research into Lost Knowledge Organization, Wellingborough, 1977

Bond, Maurice, *The Romance of St George's Chapel, Windsor*, The Society of Friends of St George's Chapel, Windsor, 1978

Bosanquet, Henry, *The Life and Death of the English Town*, The Land of Cokaygne, Cambridge, 1973

Bosanquet, Henry (illustrated by Henry Bosanquet and Nigel Pennick), *Walks Round Vanished Cambridge: Petty Cury*, Cambridge History Agency, Cambridge, 1974

Bosanquet, Henry (illustrated by Henry Bosanquet and Slim Smith), *Walks Round Vanished Cambridge: The Lion Yard*, Cambridge History Agency, Cambridge, 1974

Brett, David, *On Decoration*, The Lutterworth Press, Cambridge, 1992

Bucklow, Spike, *The Alchemy of Paint*, Marion Boyars, London & New York, 2009

Calkins, Robert G., *Monuments of Medieval Art*, E.P. Dutton, New York, 1979

Carpenter, Edward, *The Art of Creation: Essays on the Self and its Powers*, London, 1904

Carter, Thomas John Proctor, *King's College Chapel: Notes on its*

History and Present Condition, Macmillan & Co., London and Cambridge, 1867

Charpentier, Louis (trans. Sir Ronald Fraser), *The Mysteries of Chartres Cathedral*, Research Into Lost Knowledge Organisation, London, 1972

Clifton-Taylor, Alec, *The Cathedrals of England*, Thames & Hudson, London, 1967

Cobb, Gerald, *The Old Churches of London*, B.T. Batsford, London, 1948

Colledge, Eric (ed.), *The Mediaeval Mystics of England*, John Murray, London, 1962

Cook, G.H., *The English Mediaeval Parish Church*, Phoenix House, London, 1954

Critchlow, Keith, *Order in Space*, Thames & Hudson, London, 1969

Crook, Alec C., *From the Foundation to Gilbert Scott: A History of the Buildings of St John's College, Cambridge 1511 to 1885*, St John's College, Cambridge, 1980

Crossley, F.H., *English Church Design*, B.T. Batsford, London, 1945

Crowe, Norman, *Nature and the Idea of a Man-Made World: An Investigation into the Evolutionary Roots of Form and Order in the Built Environment*, Massachusetts Institute of Technology Press, Cambridge, Mass., 1995

Cunningham, W., *Notes on the Organization of the Mason's Craft in England*, The British Academy, London, 1913

Durandus, William (trans. John Mason Neale and Benjamin Webb), *The Symbolism of Churches and Church Ornaments: A Translation of the First Book of the Rationale Divinorum Officiorum*, Gibbings & Co., London, 1893

Fernee, Ben, *Geomantic Survivals in York*, Northern Earth Mysteries, Kingston upon Hull, 1985

Fitchen, J, *The Construction of Gothic Cathedrals*, Clarendon Press, Oxford, 1961

Fulcanelli, *Le Mystere des Cathedrales*, Neville Spearman, St Helier, 1971

Gettings, Fred, *Dictionary of Occult, Hermetic and Alchemical Sigils*, Routledge & Kegan Paul, London, 1981

Ghyka, Matila, *The Geometry of Art and Life*, Dover Publications, New York, 1977

Golvers, Noel, 'De recuiteringstocht van M. Martini, S.J. door de Lage Landen in 1654 over geomantische kompassen, Chinese verzamelingen, lichtbeelden en R.P. Wilhelm van Aelst, S.J.', *De zeventiende eeuw* 10 (1994), 331-350

Gordon, Elizabeth Oke, *Prehistoric London: Its Mounds and Circles*, The Covenant Publishing Co., London, 1925

Hancox, Joy, *The Byrom Collection*, Jonathan Cape, London, 1992

Harvey, John, 'Medieval Design', *Transactions of the Ancient Monuments Society*, N.S. 6, 1958, 64–5

Harvey, John, *The Gothic World, 1100–1600: A Survey of Architecture and Art*, Harper & Row, New York, 1969

Haslehurst, Ernest, & Barwell, Noel, *Cambridge*, Blackie & Son, London, Glasgow and Bombay, n.d. (c. 1912)

Hewett, Cecil Alec, *The Development of Carpentry 1200–1700*, David & Charles, Newton Abbot, 1969

Holm, Jean, & Bowker, John (eds.), *Sacred Place*, Cassell, London, 1994

Holt, Elizabeth Gilmore, *A Documentary History of Art*, Vol.1, Doubleday Anchor Books, New York, 1957

Huxtable, Ada Louise, *The Unreal America: Architecture and Illusion*, The New Press, New York, 1997

Johnson, K.R., *The Fulcanelli Phenomenon*, Neville Spearman, St Helier, 1980

Kruft, Hanno-Walter, *Geschichte der Architekturtheorie: Von der Antike bis zur Gegenwart*, Verlag C.H. Beck, Munich, 1985

Lauweriks, J.L.M., *De ladder von het zijn*, Amsterdam, 1904

Lawlor, Robert, *Sacred Geometry: Philosophy and Practice*, Thames & Hudson, 1982

Lethaby, William R., *Architecture, Mysticism and Myth*, London 1891

Lethaby, William R., *Form in Civilisation; Collected Papers on Art and Labour*, Oxford University Press, Oxford, 1922

Littlechild, W.P., *A Short Account of King's College Chapel*, W. Heffer & Sons Ltd., Cambridge, 1921

Loftie, the Rev. W.J., *A Brief Account of Westminster Abbey*, Seeley and Co., London, 1894

MacDonald, William I., *The Pantheon: Design, Meaning and Progeny*, Harvard University Press, Cambridge, Mass., 1976

Male, Emile, *Religious Art in France, XIII Century: A Study in Mediaeval Iconography and its Sources of Inspiration*, J.M. Dent & Sons, London, 1913

Malden, Henry, *An Account of King's College Chapel in Cambridge*, Fletcher & Hodson, Cambridge, 1769

March, Lionel, *Architectonics of Humanis: Essays on Number in Architecture*, Academy Editions, Chichester, 1998

McFadzean, Patrick: 'Heraldry and Planetary Colours', *The Symbol* 4 (1984), 19-20

McFadzean, Patrick, 'Late Fragments of Ancient Mysteries', *Northern Earth Mysteries* 26 (1984), 3-11

Michell, John, *City of Revelation*, Garnstone Press, London, 1972

Mitchell, Ena, *Notes on the History of Four Cambridge Commons*, Call Printing Group, Cambridge and St Ives, 1985

Mowl, Tim, & Earnshaw, Brian: *John Wood: Architect of Obsession*, Millstream Books, Bath, 1988

Nasr, Seyyed Hossein, *Islamic Science: An Illustrated Study*, World of Islam Festival Publishing Company, Tehran, 1976

Norberg-Schulz, Christian, *Genius Loci: Towards a Phenomenology of Architecture*, Rizzoli, New York, 1980

Pennick, Nigel, 'Geomancy', *Walrus* 8, 1971, 3-5

Pennick, Nigel, 'Ex Cathedra', *Arcana, A Magazine of Cambridge Occult Lore*, February 1972, 7

Pennick, Nigel, 'The Church of St Nicholas & Our Lady in Cambridge, 1446-1968' *Arcana, A Magazine of Cambridge Occult Lore*, August 1972, 24-31

Pennick, Nigel, 'The Numerical Lore of King's College Chapel, Cambridge', *The Oracle of Albion* 3 (1972), 4-5

Pennick, Nigel, *Geomancy*, The Cokaygne Press, Cambridge, 1973

Pennick, Nigel, *The Mysteries of King's College Chapel*, First edition, The Cokaygne Press, Cambridge, 1974; second edition, Thorsons, Wellingborough, 1978, second impression, Aquarian, Wellingborough, 1982

Pennick, Nigel, *East Anglian Geomancy*, Megalithic Visions Antiquarian Papers No. 7, Bar Hill, 1975

Pennick, Nigel, 'King's College Chapel – The Hidden Message', in *The Geomancy of Cambridge* (ed. Nigel Pennick), The Institute of Geomantic Research, Cambridge, 1977, 12-16

Pennick, Nigel, 'Masonic Arts at Guildford', *Journal of Geomancy* Vol. 3 No. 3 (1979), 73-76

Pennick, Nigel, *The Ancient Science of Geomancy*, Thames & Hudson, London, 1979

Pennick, Nigel (ed.), *The Grand Mystery: Being a Reprint of Two Tracts of the Eighteenth Century on the Secrets of Free-Masonry*, Fenris-Wolf, Bar Hill, 1980

Pennick, Nigel, *The Geomancy of Glastonbury Abbey*, Fenris-Wolf, Bar Hill, 1983

Pennick, Nigel, *Trams in Cambridge*, Electric Traction Publications, Cambridge, 1983

Pennick, Nigel, 'Triangular Lodge, Rushton', *The Symbol* 1, (1983), 2-6

Pennick, Nigel, 'Parametric Diagrams', in *The Byrom Collection*, by Hancox, Joy, Jonathan Cape, London, 1992, Appendix One, 291 - 292

Pennick, Nigel, *Anima Loci*, Nideck, Bar Hill, 1993

Pennick, Nigel, *Sacred Geometry*, (1980), Capall Bann, Chieveley, 1994

Pennick, Nigel, *Celtic Sacred Landscapes*, Thames & Hudson, London, 1996

Pennick, Nigel, *Beginnings: Geomancy, Builders' Rites and Electional Astrology in the European Tradition*, Capall Bann Publishing, Chieveley, 1999

Pennick, Nigel, *On the Spiritual Arts and Crafts*, The Library of the European Tradition, Cambridge, 2001

Pennick, Nigel, *Masterworks: Arts and Crafts of Traditional Buildings in Northern Europe*, Heart of Albion Press, Wymeswold, 2002

Pennick, Nigel, *The Sacred Art of Geometry: Temples of the Phoenix*, Spiritual Arts and Crafts Publishing, Bar Hill, 2005

Pennick, Nigel, & Gout, Prof. M., *Sacrale Geometrie: Verborgen Linien in de Bouwkunst*, Synthese, Den Haag, 2004

Pennick, Nigel, *In Field and Fen*, Lear Books, Earl Shilton, 2011

Powell, Bill, 'God Ltd. Halfway between Jehovah and Mammon stands King's College Chapel', *Arcana, A Magazine of Cambridge Occult Lore*, February 1972, 9

Royal Commission on Historical Monuments England, *An Inventory of the Historical Monuments in the City of Cambridge*, 2 vols., Her Majesty's Stationery Office, London, 1959

Rushworth, Philip, 'Reflections Upon the Use of Geometry in Geomancy', *Northern Earth Mysteries* 6 (1980), 7-17

Rykwert, Joseph, *The Dancing Column: On Order in Architecture*, Massachusetts Institute of Technology Press, Cambridge, Mass., 1996

Saltmarsh, John, *Carving in King's Chapel*, King's College, Cambridge, 1970

Schoenmaekers, M.H.J., *Het Nieuwe Wereldbeeld*, Bussum 1915

Scott, W.S., *The Fantasticks*, John Westhouse, London, 1945

Shelby, L.R., *John Rogers: Tudor Military Engineer*, The Clarendon Press, Oxford, 1967

Silkstone, Thomas, *Religion, Symbolism and Meaning*, Bruno Cassirer, Oxford, 1968

Smith, Jonathan Z., *To Take Place: Toward Theory in Ritual*, University of Chicago Press, Chicago, 1987

Stirling, William, *The Canon: An Exposition of the Pagan Mystery Perpetuated in the Cabala as the Rule of All the Arts*, (1987), Garnstone Press, London, 1974

Stuart, Cecil, *Gothic Architecture*, Longmans, London, 1961

Svendsen, Peter Juhl, *Rundetarn Opklaret: Katedralens Mysterium*, Sphinx, Copenhagen, 1987

Terry, Quinlan, 'Seven Misunderstandings about Classical Architecture', in *Quinlan Terry: Selected Works, Architectural Monographs* No. 27, Academy Editions, London, 1993, 129-130

Trilling, James, *The Language of Ornament*, Thames & Hudson, London, 2001

Van der Laan, Dom H. (trans. Padovan, Richard), *Architectonic Space*, E.J. Brill, Leiden, 1983

Vitruvius (Marcus Vitruvius Pollo), trans. Morgan, Morris Hicky, *The Ten Books on Architecture*, Harvard University Press, Cambridge, Mass., 1914

Von der Dunk, Thos. H., 'Hoe klassiek is de Gothek', *Vijfentachtigste Jaarboek van het Genootschap Amstelodamum* (1993), 49-90

White, Gleeson, *The Cathedral Church of Salisbury; A Description of its Fabric and a Brief History of the See of Sarum*, G. Bell & Sons, London, 1911

Wither, George, *A Collection of Emblemes, Ancient and Moderne* (1635), Scolar Press, London, 1968

Withers, Hartley, *The Cathedral Church of Canterbury: A Description of its Fabric and a Brief History of the Archiepiscopal See*, George Bell & Sons, London, 1899

Wittkower, Rudolf, *Architectural Principles in the Age of Humanism*, (1949) Academy Editions, Chichester, 1998

Yates, Frances A., *The Art of Memory*, Routledge & Kegan Paul, London, 1966

King's College Chapel east front, August 2011

About the Author

Nigel Pennick was born in 1946 in Guildford, Surrey, and spent his childhood in London and Essex. A graduate of London University, he qualified in the biological sciences, and worked in scientific research for fifteen years in Cambridge, with periods at the Université Libre de Bruxelles, Belgium and the University of Guelph, Canada. During this time he published twenty-nine scientific papers that described eight new species of marine algae. In parallel with his scientific work, he also participated in folk traditions and the scene in Cambridge, and in 1985 he became a full-time writer and lecturer on history and folklore.

In 1975, he founded the Institute of Geomantic Research, which published a journal and a number of papers on all aspects of geomancy and earth mysteries. In the late 1970s and early 80s he organized six geomantic conferences in Cambridge and nearby towns, and from the mid-1980s to the late 90s he travelled widely and gave lectures and workshops in Ireland, Holland, Germany, Switzerland, Austria and the United States as well as in Great Britain. He has also organized and participated in several spiritual tours of ancient sacred places in England, Wales and Ireland, and written books on a range of subjects, including runes, mythology, geomancy, ley lines, labyrinths, Celtic art and landscapes, traditional rites and ceremonies, folk magic and the histories of certain underground railways in London.

He is also an artist in traditional media and stained glass, and has illustrated many of his books. In 2011 a one-man show of his Visionary Steeples artwork was held at Emmanuel Church, Cambridge. He plays with The Traditional Music of Cambridgeshire Collective and participates in the traditional calendar customs of Cambridgeshire. In 2009 he restored the custom of parading the May Day Garland through Cambridge.

www.ingramcontent.com/pod-product-compliance
Ingram Content Group UK Ltd.
Pitfield, Milton Keynes, MK11 3LW, UK
UKHW020615180726
13836UKWH00010B/2481

9 781904 658580